Faith in the Game

ALSO BY TOM OSBORNE

More Than Winning
On Solid Ground

TOM OSBORNE

Faith in the Game

LESSONS ON FOOTBALL, WORK, AND LIFE

Broadway Books
New York

WaterBrook Press
Colorado Springs

A hardcover edition of this book was published in 1999
by Broadway Books and WaterBrook Press.
The quote on page 20, from "The Road Not Taken" by Robert Frost,
is from *The Poetry of Robert Frost,* edited by Edward Connery Lathem. Copyright 1944 by
Robert Frost. Copyright © 1969 by Henry Holt and Co., LLC.
Reprinted by permission of Henry Holt & Co., LLC.

This book is copublished with WaterBrook Press, 2375 Telstar, Suite 160,
Colorado Springs, CO 80920, a division of Random House, Inc.

Churches, youth groups, and ministries please call 1-800-603-7051, ext. 232, at
WaterBrook Press for volume discounts and special sales information.

Broadway Books titles may be purchased for business or promotional use or for special
sales. For information, please write to: Special Markets Department, Random House, Inc.,
1540 Broadway, New York, NY 10036.

Visit our website at www.broadwaybooks.com

First trade paperback edition published 2000.

The Library of Congress has cataloged the hardcover edition as:
Osborne, Tom, 1937–
Faith in the game: lessons on football, work, and life / by
Tom Osborne.—1st ed.
p. cm.
1. Osborne, Tom, 1937– 2. Football coaches—United States
Biography. 3. Conduct of life. I. Title
GV939.O77 A33 1999
796.332'092—dc21
[B]
99-32557

Designed by Tina Thompson

ISBN 0-7679-0423-0
WaterBrook ISBN 1-57856-392-5
00 01 02 03 04 10 9 8 7 6 5 4 3 2 1

Contents

Acknowledgments

I would like to thank my wife, Nancy, and my children, Mike, Ann, and Suzanne, for gracefully bearing the burden of having a husband and father who was too often in the public eye and too often gone. I would also like to thank the University of Nebraska coaches and players who taught me so much about competition, discipline, and caring. My student assistant, Leslie Barnes, provided invaluable help in putting this book together. Rita Ude, my assistant, was very helpful typing and correcting the manuscript. Both Leslie and Rita were able to make it appear that my command of the English language is considerably better than it actually is.

Introduction

In July 1997, I informed Frank Solich, my assistant head coach, that I anticipated the 1997 season would be my last. I had made some personal and professional commitments contingent upon stepping aside as head football coach for the University of Nebraska Cornhuskers that I believed needed to be honored. My major concern, however, was whether or not the university administration would promote Frank to the head coaching position. If there was a desire to hire from outside the staff, I would not resign, as I believed strongly in the importance of staff continuity. I did not want to leave the coaches and players with a new coach who might make changes in staff or philosophy that would be disruptive to the program.

Early in the season, I met with Bill Byrne, our athletic director, and James Moeser, the chancellor of the University of Nebraska–Lincoln, to share what I was thinking. They seemed surprised by my decision to step aside and asked that I give it further thought. They did not, however, express any serious objection to the possibility of Frank's being named head coach.

As the season unfolded, I experienced conflicting emotions. I felt that it was important to do what I had said I was going to do, yet I kept hoping that something might come up that would necessitate my staying on. I wasn't ready to quit, yet I didn't feel right about committing to something and then not following through. Each game we played, each stadium we visited, had special meaning. Rather than coaching each game to try to win it and get it behind us, I found myself paying more attention to the physical setting, the preparation of the players as they taped, dressed, and went through their pregame rituals. I also was more aware of my emotions as the time for another kickoff approached. It was an eerie feeling to know that something that had been such a big part of my life was drawing to a close, yet the season continued to unfold with the same rhythms that so many others had.

I could relate to what former Michigan coach Bo Schembechler wrote after his last season:

> "Take a good last look," I whispered to myself. Fans were cheering and throwing roses. My players were slapping hands as they counted down the clock. "NINE! EIGHT! SEVEN! . . ."
>
> Take a good last look. Somehow, on that field, at that moment, with the Big Ten title about to come our way, with another trip to Pasadena guaranteed, with my guys sweaty and bloody and whooping it up and the whole stadium on its feet—". . . SIX! FIVE! FOUR! . . ."—somehow, I knew I would never be back.
>
> This would be my last game at Michigan Stadium.

I knew what Bo was talking about. Each game that we played was poignant for me, as I knew that I would not be coaching a Nebraska team against that opponent again.

Our game against the University of Missouri on November 8, 1997, was particularly memorable. We were trailing by a touchdown late in the game and Missouri had the football. We finally forced them to punt and gained possession of the football with less than a minute remaining and no time-outs left. Our quarterback, Scott Frost, orchestrated a drive that culminated with a great diving catch in the end zone by freshman Matt Davison. The ball bounced off another receiver, Shevin Wiggins, was kicked in the air, and Matt dove and barely got his hands under the ball to tie the game. We went on to win 45–38 in overtime. It was a miraculous win that enabled us to remain undefeated with a chance of still winning the national championship.

Sometime during the week following the Missouri game, I noticed something was physically wrong with me. I normally jogged three miles after practice or spent thirty minutes on the StairMaster. I found that I could get only halfway through a workout and then became so fatigued I could no longer continue. The first time this happened, I rationalized it by reflecting on the fact that I had been putting in long hours and was a little tired. Then it happened the next night and the next, and I knew that something was really wrong.

I made it through the rest of the week. We beat Iowa State

soundly in our last home game, on Saturday, November 15. When we introduced the seniors to the crowd and they ran out on the field for the last time in Lincoln, a great many had tears in their eyes. I had a few in mine, as well. I got through the postgame interviews, did my TV show, and then checked myself into the Bryan Hospital emergency room at about ten o'clock that night.

It didn't take long for the doctors to diagnose my problem as atrial fibrillation, a condition in which the upper chamber of the heart beats erratically and does not empty properly. The condition was not immediately life-threatening but could result in a blood clot or stroke if left untreated. The next morning I was given an anesthetic and Dr. Krueger, a personal physician, was able to shock my heart back into a normal rhythm. I returned to work later that afternoon but was still pretty weak.

This was a significant event, because I took it as part of the answer to the question of what I needed to do in regard to stepping aside. The doctor had said that the atrial fibrillation would probably reoccur at some point, was likely related to stress, and sometimes becomes a permanent condition that one must learn to live with.

I prayed about what I needed to do and could never feel comfortable spiritually with any solution but to quit coaching. It seemed I was being told that it was time to do something other than coach. Having already had heart bypass surgery 12 years earlier, I took the latest episode with my heart as the final answer to my dilemma. Part of me wanted to stay in coaching, but from that point on I knew that my coaching days at Nebraska were about over.

I met with Bill Byrne and Chancellor Moeser again a few days before our Big 12 playoff game with Texas A&M on December 6. I told them that I was sure the right thing for me to do, at this point in my life, was to step aside.

I once again expressed to them my confidence in Frank Solich. Frank was stable, well organized, and a good communicator. He knew football and knew what would work in Nebraska. I was sure that Frank would hold the staff together and would take good care of the players. Fortunately, there was no administrative disagreement.

On December 10, 1997, I informed the coaches during our

morning staff meeting that I was leaving and that Frank would be taking over. I told the players later that afternoon, and a short while later I held a press conference officially announcing the change. This was, without a doubt, the longest day of my coaching career. I loved those players and coaches; telling them I was leaving was very painful.

A few players spoke at the press conference. I don't remember exactly what they said, but I can remember our fullback Joel Mackovica, quarterback Scott Frost, offensive lineman Matt Hoskinson, and tight end Vershan Jackson saying a few words, indicating that they would miss having me around. My wife, Nancy, was there. She had put up with a lot over 36 years of coaching and was her usual supportive self. I said a few words, introduced Frank Solich, and that was it. I am known for my stoic demeanor, but I can assure you, it was all that I could do to maintain my composure. I had been involved with organized football since I was in the eighth grade, and all of my professional life had been devoted to the game. My personal identity was intertwined with coaching. I loved the game, the players, and the coaches. Resigning constituted a major shift in my life. Some things would never be the same again.

Since stepping down, I have frequently been asked about the success of the Nebraska football program. Many people have expressed interest in two major facets of the program: (1) 36 years of consistency, and (2) five particularly outstanding years, from 1993 to 1997.

Since my predecessor Bob Devaney came to Nebraska in 1962, there has never been a losing season. From 1969 through 1998, Nebraska had at least nine or more wins each season and went to a bowl game each year during that 30-year period. This level of consistency has been unparalleled in NCAA annals. The last five years of my coaching career at Nebraska, the school's record was 60 wins and 3 losses. We won three national championships in the five-year period and came very close to a fourth when we missed a field goal at the conclusion of the 1994 Orange Bowl to lose to Florida State 18–16.

In reflecting on our football success, I believe it is important to examine five factors that contribute to a strong football program. They are: (1) good facilities, (2) tradition, (3) coaching,

(4) a large population base from which to recruit, and (5) good weather, particularly good weather during the recruiting season.

Nebraska is in good shape regarding the first three factors. Our facilities are among the best in the country, our football tradition is outstanding, and we have an excellent group of coaches. We don't fare well in regard to the other two variables, however. We are unusual among most major football programs in that we do not have a large population base. Only 1.6 million people live in the state of Nebraska, and adjacent states are not densely populated. We do not have great weather in December, January, and February, when most recruiting visits occur; instead we generally have snow and very cold weather. We often have recruits who have never seen snow before arrive in the middle of a blizzard. Needless to say, this makes recruiting difficult, and consistently our recruiting classes have not been ranked among the top classes nationally. We often were not rated in the top 10, or even the top 20.

But if you look at our record, you'll see that Nebraska ranked among the top 25 teams in the nation for 30 consecutive years, from 1969 through 1998, and 21 times we ranked in the top 10. We have generally performed much better on the field than our recruiting-class rankings would indicate. If there is any validity to the ratings of the recruiting gurus, our coaches and support staff have been able to maximize the talents of our players to an unusual degree.

One of the most helpful concepts that I came across in my coaching career did not come from someone in football. It came, rather, from John Wooden, the former UCLA basketball coach. In his book, *They Call Me Coach,* John mentioned that he never talked to his players about winning. He emphasized proper technique, effort, conditioning, and teamwork. He believed if a team prepared properly, winning would take care of itself. Focusing on the process is more important than concentrating on the end result.

A fan once told me, as we prepared to play an important game against Oklahoma, that I needed to find some way to "inflame" our players so that we might win. As the years went by, I became increasingly convinced that John Wooden knew more than the fan did. Pregame speeches and motivational gimmicks were not nearly as important as daily work on footwork, ball handling, blocking, tackling, and all of the fundamentals that translate into playing well. Winning was seen as a by-product of sound preparation. As Sun Tzu said centuries ago, "Victory is achieved before, not just during, the battle."

We have been able to do some things at Nebraska that have enabled us to optimize potential to an unusual degree. Hopefully, these principles and practices that have been effective in developing a strong football program will interest fans and also have some application beyond the athletic field. A strong football organization often has similarities to businesses and other organizations involved in a competitive arena.

After spending a year away from the game and having gained the perspective that time and distance often provide, my thoughts continue to gravitate toward issues of character. Much of what was accomplished at Nebraska sprang from a unique team atmosphere that revolved around attitudes and relationships associated with character. We had many people of faith involved in our organization, and spiritual factors were an integral part of how issues related to character were perceived.

Quite often books of this nature are the creation of a professional writer who has based his work on a few interviews with the "author" of the book. That has not been the case with this book. The thoughts expressed are mine, written in my own words. Writing this book has been a somewhat therapeutic process. It provided a formal sense of closure to my experience as a football coach at the University of Nebraska.

Faith in the Game

■ 1 ■
Character

Be more concerned with your character than your reputation,
because your character is what you really are;
your reputation is merely what others think you are.
—John Wooden, former UCLA basketball coach

Although difficult to define, character is a basic part of life. It is the driving and defining force behind behavior. However, character has been accorded less importance in our culture recently. A number of polls taken in 1998 indicate that a substantial majority of Americans believe there is no correlation between private behavior and job performance. Since private behavior is the best indicator of character, these polls seem to indicate that we, as a nation, are not greatly concerned about character issues.

Character influences action. We often behave out of fear of the consequences of our actions, rather than out of a sense of right and wrong. English writer Thomas Macaulay once observed, "The measure of a man's real character is what he would do if he knew he would never be found out." Character springs from the heart. It relates to what we would do and how we would react if there were no consequences or social restraints to keep us in check.

Horace Greeley described the importance of character in this way: "Fame is a vapor, popularity is an accident, money takes wings, those who cheer you today may curse you tomorrow. The only thing that endures is character." Many of the things we pursue, such as popularity, money, and public approval, are very transitory. In the final analysis, the only enduring factor that we have to show for our stay on earth is the quality of our character.

Aristotle attributed character to the choices we make. He said, "Character is that which reveals moral purpose, exposing the class of things a man chooses or avoids." He believed that the essence of character is exposed by the activities and people with whom one associates. Companions have been compared to buttons on an elevator—they will either take you up or take you down. Proverbs 13:20 states: "He that walketh with wise men shall be wise; but a companion of fools shall be destroyed."

Character was once believed to be an integral part of success. In his book *The Seven Habits of Highly Effective People,* Stephen Covey finds a historical correlation between character and success. In reviewing literature related to success, Covey found that success was primarily defined by character traits for the first 150-odd years of our nation's existence: A successful person was one who was loyal, honest, kind, trustworthy, and self-sacrificing. However, Covey notes that over the last 50 years there has been a definite shift in how success is measured. Success has come to be defined to a significant degree by public image, rather than by the quality of one's character. Covey's findings suggest that our culture has moved from a reliance on character toward a preoccupation with public opinion, personality skills, and effective ways to manipulate others. The cultural shift from substance to style is reflected in the polls indicating that Americans see no relationship between private behavior and how one performs publicly.

Despite the implications of polls, not everyone dismisses character issues as being irrelevant. Warren Buffett, chairman of Berkshire Hathaway, spoke at a symposium at the University of Nebraska in 1994. He shared his experience while serving on the board of directors for Salomon Brothers, an investment banking firm. Buffett was notified on a Friday afternoon in 1991 that he had been given sole responsibility to select a new person to lead Salomon Brothers. The previous CEO had been forced to resign, and Buffett was to select his replacement within 48 hours; time was of the essence. There was concern about a possible loss of confidence in Salomon Brothers, prompting a mass exodus of investors. Buffett chose to consider a dozen candidates already high up within the Salomon Brothers organization. He relates:

> I interviewed these people serially over a three- or four-hour period. . . . I did not ask them their grades in business school. . . . I didn't even ask them if they went to business school. I

did not ask for their résumé. I never saw a résumé on the fellow that I decided on. I really had to decide in that time who was going to be the person for me to go into a foxhole with and who was going to be able to lead this organization during an extremely difficult period when people would be quitting, when customers would be badgering them, and when lenders would be pulling out . . . so in the end I picked out the individual there who I felt was an outstanding human being. . . . Now the interesting thing about that choice is that the qualities that attracted me to him were not impossible for anyone to achieve. He didn't have to be able to jump seven feet, he didn't have to be able to throw a football 60 yards, he didn't have to be able to remember every bridge hand he played the previous year or something of the sort; there was no feat of intellect or something like that. What he did was bring qualities like steadfastness and honesty. I knew he would tell me the bad news. . . . I knew that he would not get his ego involved in decisions. I knew that he would not be envious or greedy or all of those things that make people unattractive.

Mr. Buffett concluded his remarks by saying,

One friend of mine said that in hiring he looks for three things—intelligence, energy, and character. If they don't have the last one, the first two will kill you because it's true that if you go in to hire somebody that doesn't have character, you better hope they are dumb and lazy because if they are smart and energetic, they will get you into all kinds of trouble.

In a tight spot, Warren Buffett did not employ conventional hiring procedures. He didn't have time to appoint a search committee or involve a headhunter. He chose the person who displayed character qualities that set him apart from the other candidates. As one of the most effective investors of our time, Buffett has consistently emphasized character and quality of management in his decisions to buy companies. Character is not irrelevant; it is a key issue for Buffett.

Success in college football often parallels effective business practices. At the beginning of each season, approximately 15 Division I-A college football teams possess the tradition, coaching, and talent to win a national championship. The differences among these 15 teams are very slight. Quite often the factor determining who finishes first, tenth, or fifteenth is largely a matter of character. Those teams that develop a unique chemistry based on factors such as honesty, hard work, self-sacrifice, faith, and loyalty will outperform teams of comparable ability that lack those traits.

Character development starts very early in life and is aided by an intact family that is stable, caring, and grounded in a faith-based values system. The breakdown of families in the United States has contributed to a deterioration of character in today's society. Nearly one-half of our young people grow up without both biological parents. There are 18 million fatherless children in our nation, most of whom were abandoned by their fathers while infants. When a father doesn't care enough to share any part of a child's life, there is a void. In attempting to fill that void, young people often engage in antisocial and destructive behavior. They are more likely to drop out of school, abuse drugs and alcohol, parent a child out of wedlock, and engage in criminal activity. Even in families that are intact, parents spend 40 percent less time with their children than they did a generation ago.

As my coaching career progressed, I noticed that the athletes we were dealing with often had less stability and family support than players I coached in the early 1960s. The great majority of our players who had trouble obeying the law or following team rules had had virtually no parental support. Many had been on their own since childhood.

Just as young people are troubled by unstable homes, the external environment in which they live is more threatening and hostile. The United States leads developed nations in teenage homicide, suicide, and pregnancy rates. Violence among young people has grown at a frightening rate. This reality has been brought home to us: Seven athletes who were once part of our football program have been shot. The shootings occurred over a span of ten years from 1985 to 1995. Two of the young men were walk-ons who left the team for financial reasons after one year. Both were shot fatally, one in New York and one in Los Angeles. One prominent player, Abdul Muhammed, was also shot in Los Angeles and played his final two seasons with a bullet lodged in his buttock. Fullback Chris Norris was shot from behind—the bullet passing through his arm. Receiver Brendon Holbein was shot in the side but was not seriously wounded. Both Norris and Holbein were shot in Lincoln. In each of these shootings, the player was unarmed and hit by random gunfire. I cannot recall a single player being shot in the first 23 years of my coaching career at Nebraska. Times have changed.

Another hostile element we face today is drug use and abuse, and alcohol is the drug that concerns me the most. It is estimated that several million teenagers in our nation are alcoholics. Forty percent of young people who use alcohol before age 16 become addicted. Forty percent of 14- and 15-year-olds use alcohol regularly, resulting in a 16 percent addiction rate. When drinking occurs at such an early age, the disease often progresses from the first drink to alcoholism in a matter of weeks or months. Individuals who are physically and emotionally immature are more susceptible to the addictive qualities of alcohol than are those who begin drinking as adults. Young people addicted to hard drugs are a real concern but number in the hundreds of thousands, as opposed to the millions addicted to alcohol.

At least 90 percent of the serious discipline problems we had while I was head coach involved alcohol. A particularly tragic case was that of Terrell Farley. Terrell was an outstanding linebacker in 1995 and 1996. There were indications he was developing an alcohol problem, so Terrell was placed on probation and was required to enter alcohol treatment. Unfortunately, he relapsed near the end of the 1996 season and was dismissed from the team. We moved our starting safety, Mike Minter, to Terrell's linebacker slot. We then juggled others in the secondary to compensate for moving Minter. We would have been all right, except one secondary player was injured and another was sick in our Big 12 playoff game against Texas in December of 1996. The juggling we did to compensate for Terrell's absence contributed to an uncharacteristically subpar defensive performance, and we lost to Texas. The loss was painful. A victory over Texas would have enabled us to play Florida State in the Sugar Bowl for a third consecutive national championship. The suspension of one key player can make a difference, and alcohol abuse is often part of the problem. We came down hard on alcohol use and implemented a peer-enforced alcohol ban after 1992. However, the few lapses we had were often devastating to both the team and the player involved.

Compounding the problems of violence and alcohol abuse are themes in print, television, movies, and music that do not promote sound character. One very persistent message is that possessions produce happiness and fulfillment. Young people are inculcated with the idea that if they have a certain brand of tennis shoe, a specific kind of automobile, or a higher standard of living, they will be happy. However, my experience has been that those from affluent homes are often just as troubled as those from impoverished circumstances.

Another prevailing theme is that promiscuity is acceptable and without consequence. Again, such an assumption is not true. As I interacted with players and listened to their problems, I became convinced that promiscuity diminishes self-esteem and usually has negative consequences. I recall a linebacker breaking down in tears as he told of his girlfriend's abortion. He thought abortion was wrong and felt responsible for the loss of a life.

A third common false impression concerns violence. Young people witness so many violent acts on television and in movies that they become desensitized to the reality and consequences of violence. In 1998, two young boys shot several classmates in Jonesboro, Arkansas. Amazingly, they assumed they would be allowed to go back to school the next day and seemed devoid of any understanding of the enormity of what they had done. In April 1999, two teenagers killed 12 classmates, a teacher, and themselves in Littleton, Colorado. They wounded many others and apparently had planned to kill hundreds of people in their community. Violent acts of this nature have become all too common in our culture.

The promotion of alcohol as a necessity for parties, celebrations, and having a good time is also very popular in the media.

Most people in alcohol commercials are young, attractive, and vibrant. The commercials don't show the devastation that alcohol abuse causes, nor do they acknowledge alcohol abuse as a major problem with young people.

The breakdown of the family and these threatening aspects of our environment often cause young people to feel troubled and confused. Many of them have not been exposed to a solid value system in their developmental years.

Since there is no longer a consensus concerning values that were once commonly accepted, we decided to start from scratch with our athletes when they came into the football program. We systematically discussed values and character as they related to our weekly football preparation. Former Nebraska player and Kansas City Chiefs strength coach Dave Redding told me about a tradition instituted by Marty Schottenheimer, former head coach of the Kansas City Chiefs. In preparing for each game, Coach Schottenheimer emphasized a "theme of the week." Each week he focused on a specific quality he felt would be conducive to an effective performance in the Chiefs' upcoming game. The themes focused on attitude, teamwork, and demeanor.

At Nebraska, we decided to try something similar, and we approached each game from a thematic perspective. The themes we chose related to character traits we thought would promote a better team and better people. Since we normally played 12 or 13 games, we presented 12 to 13 different themes pertaining to character. In the course of a season, presenting these topics essentially provided our athletes with an extensive character-education course.

Prior to each Tuesday practice, we distributed the scouting report on our upcoming opponent. The theme of the week was included in the scouting report, along with quotes by accomplished people from Vince Lombardi to Mother Teresa relating to the theme. At Tuesday's team meeting, I discussed that week's character trait and the people we had quoted. The quotes helped our players better understand each theme and how it related to the football team.

The following themes were included in game preparation on a regular basis: honesty, loyalty, courage, unselfishness, work ethic, discipline, confidence, leadership, teamwork, mental toughness, and perseverance. For example, the theme "courage" appeared in the scouting report as:

Courage

Whenever two teams or players of equal ability play, the one with the greater courage will win.
—Pete Carril, college basketball coach

Success is never final. Failure is never fatal. It's courage that counts.
—Sam Rutigliano, NFL and college football coach

To see what is right and not do it is a lack of courage.
—Confucius, Chinese philosopher

The test of tolerance comes when we are in a majority; the test of courage comes when we are in a minority.
—Ralph Sockman, clergyman

Fatigue makes cowards of us all.
—Vince Lombardi, former Green Bay Packers coach

Each quote was discussed and amplified with the players in a team meeting. We tried to apply the quote to circumstances surrounding a young man's daily life, as well as his role in the upcoming football game. I visited with the players about factors in the upcoming game that would demonstrate courage. For example, a willingness to pay a greater physical price in terms of downfield blocking, greater pursuit on defense, and not showing fatigue to the opponent were all considered to be elements of courage.

As we discussed each theme and related it to character, we emphasized how each topic related to events both on and off the playing field. The quote from Confucius related to each player taking a stance to do the right thing rather than the common thing. When others pressure a player to engage in behavior that will reflect badly on the team, it was pointed out, standing up for one's beliefs often takes great courage. The quote from Sam

Rutigliano was interpreted as follows: We are not so concerned with whether we win or lose; what we are concerned with is how we play the game. If we play it in the right spirit and have prepared well, our performance will display courage. The quote from Ralph Sockman demonstrates the difficulty of displaying the courage of one's convictions. Moral courage is often more difficult to exercise than physical courage. Tolerance is easier than sticking one's neck out and going it alone. Vince Lombardi recognized that a player who was exhausted would reach a point where every fiber in his being would resist one more all-out effort. As fatigue sets in, the best-conditioned team displays the greatest courage in the latter stages of a game.

As I reflect on courage, quarterback Brook Berringer comes to mind. During our 1994 season, Brook sustained a collapsed lung in a game with the University of Wyoming. Brook was injured early in the game but continued to play, even though his ribs were sore and he was short of breath. The extent of the injury wasn't known until the game was over. The injury was serious; however, Brook was cleared to play the following week against a solid Oklahoma State team. In the first half, Brook was hit hard but continued to play. A halftime examination indicated that the lung had collapsed again, and the doctors would not allow him to continue playing. At that point, Brook's status for the rest of the season was questionable. Our starting quarterback, Tommie Frazier, was out for the season with blood clots in this leg, and we had a very tough game against Kansas State at Manhattan the next week. Brook was not slated to play against Kansas State, as reinjuring the lung would definitely be a season-ending injury. The first half was close, and Brook wanted to play. In the second half, the doctors reluctantly allowed him to have his wish. Brook played well and managed to avoid further injury. He played great football throughout the remainder of the year, and we had an undefeated, national championship season. The season hung in the balance in that game in Manhattan. Brook's courage and tenacity were major factors in our having the successful season we had.

Another theme that we discussed was sacrifice. In the scouting report, it was outlined as follows:

Sacrifice

What I spent I had, what I kept I lost,
what I gave I have.
—Henry Ward Bucher, clergyman

Unless a life is lived for others, it is not worth living.
—Mother Teresa

You cannot do a kindness too soon
because you never know when it will be too late.
—Ralph Waldo Emerson

Since we live in a very self-absorbed culture, the concept of sacrificing for others has become foreign to our way of thinking. The key to having a great team or a great organization is willingness to sacrifice for the welfare of others. The above quotes emphasize the importance of giving oneself, not only for the welfare of the organization but also for one's own well-being. We stressed that when the team was successful, we all were successful; when the team failed to play well, we all lost. There was a high priority placed on putting team goals ahead of personal goals. We emphasized the importance of reaching out to members of the team who were discouraged or injured. The more one gives to others, the more one receives in return.

Sacrifice is a trait that was displayed by so many players over the years that it is difficult to choose one example. The 1982 season was particularly memorable, as we had two great running backs that year, Roger Craig and Mike Rozier. They both played I-back, and, in an effort to get both of them on the field at the same time, we asked Roger to play fullback and made Mike the I-back. This decision was made because Roger was the better blocker and could play fullback, whereas Mike would not be as effective as a fullback. Playing fullback, Roger carried the ball some, but not as much as he would have at I-back. Instead, he blocked and carried the ball sparingly, but he made a great contribution, and we had a very good 12–1 season.

Since Roger was a senior and had played very well for us previously, it was hard for him to surrender much of the limelight to Mike; however, he did so with grace and was not a divisive factor when he certainly could have been. The San Francisco 49ers noticed Roger's unselfish attitude, as well as his running and blocking ability. Mike Rozier had a good NFL career; however, Roger Craig became one of the finest NFL running backs of all time. Roger's sacrifice served our team well, and, indirectly, benefited Roger also.

After first presenting the theme of the week on Tuesday, we reviewed the week's topic at the team meeting on Thursday, and I also incorporated it in my discussion with the players as part of our pregame meetings on Saturday morning. This gave the players a chance to reflect on the particular character trait relating to the theme on several occasions during the week. Over time, this began to make an impact on the way our players thought about issues relating to character. For example, as we discussed the importance of teamwork, unity, self-sacrifice, unselfishness, and loyalty, our players became much more aware of the importance of the welfare of the team. Three of our players roomed together in an apartment and had a series of parties that did not reflect well on the team. Several other players, concerned about the impact the parties were having, put an end to the partying before I heard about it.

Every Friday, our players were given a written test on the contents of the scouting report. This meant the players could not take a cursory look at the scouting report and then throw it away. They had to study it carefully in order to score well on the test.

Giving our players a weekly written examination had its genesis in 1967. Our quarterback that year was talented but occasionally threw an interception in a manner that led me to question whether he was aware of the nuances of the pass pattern that he was attempting to execute. I could not understand those occasional mental lapses. Since I was coaching the quarterbacks at that time, I decided to give a written test to the quarterbacks prior to our game at Colorado. I was surprised to see that the material we had been reviewing on the blackboard was not registering with our starting quarterback. He could not draw each pattern and describe the order in which receivers were read. Apparently, he was just looking at the whole field, trying to find somebody to throw to without a conceptual understanding of the pattern. Obviously, I had done a very poor job of teaching.

After experiencing this major breakdown in communication, I decided to administer an extensive quarterback test every week. This exam required the quarterbacks to not only draw our pass patterns correctly but to also list each of our offensive plays and to demonstrate an understanding of the audibles. Subsequently, the other position coaches began to test their players, as well. As time went on, we developed a fairly sophisticated method of teaching and testing our players. If a player could not perform well on a written test on Friday, we were reluctant to put him in a game on Saturday. Therefore, the players worked hard at the mental part of the game and we had very few players who did not have their assignments down cold by Friday afternoon. Part of their task was to be knowledgeable of character issues related to the theme of the week.

As a person grows older, it becomes more difficult to alter character. Even by the time one is in the late teenage years, personality has become somewhat intractable. I did believe, however, that our approach to presenting character issues via the theme of the week brought our team closer together. It provided a common understanding of traits essential to the success of the team. The players could not avoid thinking about matters that would make them better people and, at the same time, mold them into a better football team.

A major spiritual shift can change a person's basic character. Such changes are unpredictable and rare. It is possible, however, to influence a person's thinking about character issues by emphasizing values that relate to that person's experience. As we continued to present themes centered around team building, we began to play at a higher level. After introducing the theme-of-the-week concept, we won seven straight conference or divisional championships. Our focused discussion of character issues wasn't the only reason for our success, but it did make a major contribution.

After examining factors relevant to our team success, I know that character was the foundation. The remaining chapters of this book will deal with key components of character, the fundamental traits and attributes of sound individual and team performance. In my view, achieving an understanding of character without relating it to faith is nearly impossible. As we have struggled as a nation with separation of church and state, political correctness, relativism, and tolerance of almost anything, we have danced all around the topic of faith as an essential component of character. My experience is that our relationship to God plays a significant role in that which we call "character."

■ 2 ■
Faith

Therefore, since we are surrounded by such a great crowd of witnesses, let us throw off everything that hinders and the sin that so easily entangles, and let us run with perseverance the race marked out for us. Let us fix our eyes on Jesus, the Author and Perfector of our faith, who for the joy set before Him endured the cross scorning its shame, and sat down at the right hand of the throne of God.
—Hebrews 12:1–2

Recently, there has been a renewed interest in spirituality in the United States. Yet at the same time many areas of our culture display an anti-Christian sentiment. While omitting any reference to Christianity throughout this book may be more politically correct, and more appealing to a broad-based readership, it would not be an honest reflection of my coaching philosophy. My approach to athletics is based on Christian principles. In the competitive arena of major college football, I was more concerned with what would work rather than what would look good. I was convinced that the basic tenets of Christianity provided a solid foundation upon which to build a life—as well as a football program. The basic "building blocks" as I see them can be summarized as follows:

1. Everyone is equal in God's sight. There is no distinction on the basis of race, religion, or social position—or first, second, or third string on a football team. We are all created in God's image and are of equal value. In coaching, I tried to see each player as unique and important in God's eyes and tried to treat him accordingly.

2. Everyone has missed the mark in terms of being everything God has called him or her to be. No one is perfect, and everyone

makes mistakes. Realizing this, I tended to be more understanding of players' failings than some thought I should be.

3. Through His life, death, and resurrection, Jesus reveals the depth of God's love for each person. There is a difference between intellectually understanding that God loves you and experiencing God's love. I saw remarkable spiritual changes in players when they were fully impacted by the extent of God's love as revealed by Jesus.

4. No one is beyond redemption. With God's help, it is possible to become a different person—irrespective of past misdeeds or experiences. I never completely gave up on a player. Even though I might have dismissed him from the team, I realized that God has no deadlines and that some begin to sense his love and presence only after hitting bottom.

5. We are called to serve rather than be served. As I examined the life of Jesus, it became apparent that He came as a servant. The style of leadership I adopted, though far from perfect, was based on His model.

6. Life begins to have meaning and purpose when we choose to honor God and serve other people. Our culture indicates just the opposite—meaning and purpose derive from serving ourselves and acquiring material possessions. I tried both honoring myself and honoring God, and life seemed to make more sense when I put God first.

7. Love is more powerful than any other emotion. Coaching is often about motivating players through fear and promoting a hatred of opponents. Love among players and coaches, coupled with respect for opponents, was much more effective. God is about love, not hatred.

The apostle Paul was familiar with the Greek games and often made reference to athletics in his letters. In Hebrews 12:1–2, Paul refers to competitors in an arena, surrounded by witnesses, preparing to run a race. Spectators are an important part of athletics. I often asked our players to consider whom they played for. This question was rhetorical and needed no response; however, I wanted them to think about who was most important to them as they played the game. For some of them, the crowd provided motivation and fulfillment. They enjoyed the roar of the crowd and the adulation they received when they made a great play.

Many of them kept friends or family uppermost in their minds as they played. They wanted to please a select few who meant the most to them. Some were very aware of what professional scouts would think, as their ultimate objective was to play professional football. Others were most concerned about how the coaches would evaluate their performance. They knew the game tape would be examined closely as each play was run back and forth numerous times in the grading process. They would receive their grade on the next Monday, and this was often a traumatic experience. Some players were concerned about honoring God with their performance. They wanted their athletic abilities and achievements to reflect their faith.

I was confident that a player who was motivated primarily by his faith in God would not only give a maximum effort but also do so for the right reasons. It is easy to fool the crowd, as the crowd gets only a brief look at each play. Fans have told me what a great game a player had, when the game tapes revealed that the player had actually played very poorly. One or two plays may have stood out, but the overall quality of play was substandard. It is also easy to fool friends and family. They often don't know what the player is expected to do on each play; therefore, even those closest to the athlete are unable to evaluate his performance effectively. Fooling coaches and professional scouts is more difficult, as they are familiar with the nuances of the game and are able to review game tapes. Even coaches can be fooled, however. It is possible for a player to not fully extend when catching a pass in heavy traffic, or to take a slight loaf as he pursues the ballcarrier. The player appears to be giving maximum effort; however, he is capable of giving a little bit more. Even a coach cannot always be 100 percent accurate in his assessment of each player's effort.

The player knows and God knows what the player's motivation is on each play. There are times when a player may make a mistake in a game, yet his effort, attitude, and desire cannot be faulted. God looks on a person's heart. In my estimation, any player who attempts to honor God with his play will not give anything less than a total effort.

In the passage from Hebrews, the apostle Paul also talks about casting aside every hindrance and sin that entangles. Paul was aware that competitors in the Greek games competed naked; they literally threw aside everything that might slow them down. But he is really talking about simplifying life, stripping away attitudes, habits, and transgressions that rob us of our ability to focus on the task of running the race as God would have us run it. There is much in our culture that can drag us down and cause us to be less than we are capable of being. The negative images and false gods that appear in music, television, movies, and printed material can be destructive influences, pulling us away from what God would have us be.

A player using his athletic talent to honor God will prepare through good training habits, focused practices, and sound mental discipline in approaching a game. Many talented players never perform as they could because they do not prepare well.

Paul writes about running the race with perseverance. The Greek word we translate as "perseverance" implies a dogged determination in running a race that will not be denied. The runner is so committed and prepared that there is no possibility of failure. There is seldom a sure thing in athletics, yet Paul is referring to a level of commitment that will not fail.

Throughout my career, there were a few times I was sure our team was going to win. Irrespective of who our opponent was, the preparation was so intense and focused that I knew we would be successful. This type of assurance—spiritual—requires discipline. Prayer, meditation, scripture study, and worship are just as essential to running a successful spiritual race as physical discipline is in preparing for athletic competition.

As an observer of the Greek games, Paul wrote, "Everyone who competes in the games goes into strict training. They do it to get a crown that will not last, but we do it to get a crown that will last forever." He undoubtedly witnessed the incredible training regimen that the game participants underwent as they prepared for competition. They removed themselves from their families and went to training centers where they toiled daily for nine months in preparation for a chance to win a crown of olive branches, which would wither and turn brown in a short period of time. Paul notes that if athletes will pay such a great price for a prize of little actual value, how much more we should be willing to discipline ourselves in spiritual matters where the stakes are much higher.

In the spring of 1995, I visited Haiti with Don McClanen, the founder of the Fellowship of Christian Athletes. We saw great hardship and poverty all around us; however, our visit to one of Mother Teresa's homes for the dying was particularly memorable. This particular home was for infants and very young children, nearly all of whom were terminally ill with diseases such as AIDS. No one would care for these children except the sisters of Mother Teresa's order. These sisters had taken a vow of poverty and had no material wealth. They were allowed to visit their families once every ten years, and they worked in a setting where nearly 100 percent of their small patients died. Overwhelmed by the enormity and the hopelessness of their task, I wanted to talk to one of these sisters very badly so I could gain some sense of how they were able to go on day after day in such an environment. I was able to gain the attention of one of the sisters who spoke English and asked her how she was able to survive under such conditions. Her answer was surprisingly simple. She informed me that the sisters were given three hours a day for prayer, meditation, scripture study, and group worship. She said that practicing these spiritual disciplines renewed, energized, and sustained them. She did not seem to feel deprived or stressed but rather appeared to feel privileged to be involved in her work. Discipline gets us from point A to point B, whether we are engaged in athletics, academics, business, or spiritual matters. It is surprising how disciplined we are in many areas of our lives yet assume we will be given spiritual power without practicing spiritual discipline. In a figurative sense, we want to be 300-pound weight lifters but only want to go into the weight room on Christmas and Easter.

In Hebrews 12:2, Paul stresses the importance of where we fix our eyes. In athletics, proper vision and focus are critical factors. The baseball player's eyes must be locked on the rotation of the baseball in order to hit it. A receiver must watch the football into his hands if he is to catch it. In a spiritual sense, the eyes are equally important. Paul says the eyes should be fixed on Jesus as our model. It is important to recognize that Jesus came as a servant, not as a king. In coaching, there is often a temptation for the coach to see himself as the ultimate authority and the athletes as being subservient. If Jesus is the model, then the coach is truly a servant of his players. He may be a disciplinarian and stern at times; however, his primary motivation from a spiritual perspective is to serve and to care for those with whom he has been entrusted.

Paul was a Roman citizen, but his thought was heavily influenced by Greek culture. During the peak of Greek civilization, there was great emphasis placed on symmetry and balance. The Greeks believed an educated person was one who had developed himself along three dimensions: physical, mental, and spiritual. A person who had grown and developed in all three areas was deemed to be an educated person because of the balance he was able to achieve in his life.

Given the Greek emphasis on balancing mind, body, and spirit, I was particularly intrigued by some statistics released a few years ago by the National Football League Players Association. The figures indicated that the average playing career in the National Football League was slightly more than three years, a significant number of players had no money upon leaving the NFL, and the divorce rate and other personal problems were significant. This information indicates that professional football might not be as desirable a career as many believe. I was concerned about this, particularly since the focus of so many of our players was to play in the NFL. Many believed that a professional football experience would be the answer to their prayers.

In the United States, the essence of the "American dream" is to have money, celebrity status, youth, and talent. Nearly all of the players in the National Football League are well paid, enjoy celebrity status, are young, and are very talented. It has been disturbing to see how many of our former players, who at age 22 or 23 appeared to have the "American dream" as they entered the National Football League, left the league with broken dreams and disillusionment a few years later.

Many professional football players are excellent athletes but have ignored intellectual and spiritual growth. They know how to block and tackle but are limited to athletic excellence. Still others have done well athletically and intellectually, many having earned college degrees. Players who have grown only in their physical and intellectual capabilities still lack balance in their lives if they have no spiritual commitment. Eventually, an injury occurs or the legs and reflexes fail, and the cheering stops. For those players who had no spiritual dimension in their lives, the end of their athletic careers often ushered in a period of bewilderment and confusion. All that their lives had been based upon suddenly crumbled when they no longer had a football career.

An extreme example of the difficulty in transitioning from the NFL to ordinary life is that of an acquaintance who had had a long and successful professional career. Upon his retirement from the NFL, he had a difficult time finding a place in the business world. Each morning he would leave his home in a business suit with his briefcase, and each evening he would return, giving every appearance to his family that things were going well. However, he was actually sitting all day long in a parked car in despair over his inability to fit into the business community. He eventually took his own life and that of his wife, as well. This case was more sensational than most; however, it does illustrate the confusion and despair many encounter upon leaving professional athletics.

We emphasized the important role that spiritual inquiry and development would play in each player's experience at the university. Once I read Robert Frost's poem "The Road Not Taken" to the team. The poem began:

> *Two roads diverged in a yellow wood,*
> *And sorry I could not travel both*
> *And be one traveler, long I stood*
> *And looked down one as far as I could*
> *To where it bent in the undergrowth;*
>
> *And both that morning equally lay*
> *In leaves no step had trodden black.*
> *Oh, I kept the first for another day!*
> *Yet knowing how way leads on to way,*
> *I doubted if I should ever come back.*

Reading Robert Frost may seem like a strange thing for a college football coach to do. However, I was trying to point out that choices often represent a fork in the road of life. Two paths may be very close together at the initial decision point but grow farther apart as life progresses. I wanted the players to consider the direction their life was taking, not just intellectually and athletically, but spiritually as well. Decisions made early in life have far-reaching ramifications. Decisions of a spiritual nature are the most important decisions.

Many successful coaches have been people of faith. Tom Landry, former coach of the Dallas Cowboys, indicates that a major factor in his career was faith. He says in his autobiography, "Knowing your job isn't the most important thing in your life relieves a lot of the pressure. And because I felt I was doing God's will for my life, I knew I didn't have to do it all in my own strength."

One of the difficult aspects of coaching is that your life's work is done weekly in a very public place. A great many people, ranging from sportswriters to fans, believe they know precisely what moves the coach should make. It becomes apparent that life in such a goldfish bowl is often packed with pressure and criticism.

There were times when I was perceived as "too nice" to be a good football coach. Each time we lost the "big one," there were those who thought my being a person of faith was a major part of the problem.

From God's perspective, who wins or loses a football game is not a major issue. Tom Landry's quote refers to the fact that God calls us to be faithful, He does not require us to be successful. The coach does not have to carry the whole burden alone.

John Wooden was possibly the greatest coach of all time. John coached UCLA to ten NCAA basketball championships with faith at the heart of both his personal life and his coaching philosophy. John wrote, "Sometimes I wonder if the good Lord isn't almost as much the coach as I am." He consistently acknowledged the role his spiritual life played during his coaching career. I am not big on autographs; however, one of my most prized possessions is a basketball autographed by John Wooden.

My friend Bobby Bowden has compiled an amazing record as Florida State's football coach. More important though, Bobby is thoroughly grounded in his faith and has set a great Christian example through his coaching. We played Bobby's team several times—usually without much success. At no time have I ever known Bobby to act in a way that was inconsistent with the faith he professes.

Bobby made the following statement concerning his spiritual life:

> The biggest way in which my style of leadership has changed over the years—and I'm talking about 41 years of coaching— is that I live my life more Christian-patterned than it was when I got started in this. At least I hope I have grown in my Christian life through the years. I've tried to be a better example to my players.

Bobby and his staff begin their coaches' meeting each morning with a short devotional period, much as we have done at Nebraska. It is interesting to note that two of the most successful football programs in the 1980s and 1990s started each day in this manner. The common perception of football coaches is that of hard-driving, profane, callous individuals who care little about spiritual matters. Often people engaged in highly competitive enterprises believe that matters of faith hinder effective performance. My experience has led me to believe that spiritual preparation contributes to effective performance no matter what the arena.

Many coaches have enjoyed short-term success while ignoring spiritual commitment. However, a high percentage of coaches who had lengthy careers have been people of faith. Faith has provided them with a compass to find their way through the pitfalls of coaching.

Training only the mind and muscles for an athletic contest without preparing emotionally and spiritually is often not very effective. The heart sustains the mind and the muscles. Those who attempt to achieve challenging goals operating solely on a physical and mental plane, with no spiritual depth, are analogous to a body functioning without a heart.

Faith appears to correlate with physical health. Dr. Ken Cooper, founder of the aerobics fitness movement, studied the effects of faith on general well-being. In his book *It's Better to Believe*, Dr. Cooper observes that intrinsic belief is "characterized by such qualities as profound spiritual commitment, a sense of having found the ultimate meaning of life, a devotion to heartfelt prayer, and a quest for a truly transformed life. This kind of inner conviction—which may be accompanied by, but is never limited to, outward external observance—is the key to real spiritual power. Furthermore, intrinsic belief has the capacity to spark major personal enrichment in every area of life—including dramatic improvements in physical health, emotional well-being, and levels of fitness." Dr. Cooper also refers to a body of research suggesting that authentic faith contributes to less depression, a lower incidence of cancer, less cardiovascular disease, and healthier emotional balance.

Pollster George Gallup, Jr., concluded in his book *The Saints Among Us* that approximately 13 percent of Americans live their lives out of a deep, authentic, spiritual commitment. He found that these "saints" were more compassionate, less prejudiced, more conscious of God's presence, and led happier and more joyful lives.

I rise at 5:30 A.M. each day and spend 45 minutes in prayer, meditation, and the scriptures, and I have found that this has become the most important part of my day. Although there were times when I failed to exercise principles of my faith, a daily time of spiritual preparation enabled me to be more consistent in my Christian walk. Just as it is very difficult to perform athletically without adequate strength training, it is unlikely that one can possess spiritual power and not practice the disciplines of prayer, scripture reading, and regular worship. Often during preparation for a particularly important game, it was convenient to maintain that I was "too busy" to prepare spiritually, as well. There was often not enough time in the day to prepare thoroughly for an opponent, particularly a powerful one. I often felt self-imposed pressure to watch more film, think of all eventualities, and spend more time in meetings. However, I learned over time that the more pressure I was under, the less I could afford to ignore my spiritual life.

We started our staff meetings each day at 7 A.M. The first activity of the day was a short devotional period that usually lasted no more than ten minutes. Several of our coaches felt comfortable reading a verse of scripture and then leading a brief discussion of how that scripture related to our team and our daily lives. We rotated responsibility for leadership of the devotional period daily. The devotional period ended with a short time of silent prayer that allowed us to focus on what God would have us do that day. Attendance at the devotional period was optional. Even though no one was obligated to participate, nearly all of our coaches attended.

The devotional period served to focus our thoughts on God and to put the day's activities in a better spiritual perspective. We had times when there was disagreement among the staff, and there were often difficulties with players. Conflict is inevitable in coaching. However, the devotional period at the beginning of the day set a tone that decreased the amount of tension and discord. The more we united to serve one Master, the more distractions and animosities fell away.

The morning of every game, I prayed for the players and coaches individually. I asked that the players would be strengthened, sustained, have a sense of God's presence, and that they might be spared injury. I prayed that each coach might recognize and understand what God would have him do that day. I also lifted up our opponents in prayer, asking that they might be spared injury and that both teams would glorify God with their play.

Some might believe that taking time to pray is an exercise in futility; however, there is a body of research by Larry Dossey (1997) and others indicating a real, demonstrable power in prayer. For example, patients who are prayed for generally improve more quickly and have better chances of surviving than patients who are not prayed for. Dr. Steve Carveth, one of the surgeons who performed my heart surgery in 1985, told me that he tried to pray as often as he could before surgery. He noticed that those patients he was able to pray for usually did better than those he didn't pray for. As I received the anesthetic prior to the surgery, I was hoping Steve hadn't forgotten to pray. I had confidence in the surgeons, but certainly wouldn't object if God had His hand in the matter, as well.

The morning of each game we provided an opportunity for the players to attend either a chapel service or a mass. Services lasted a half hour, and attendance was voluntary. Approximately two-thirds of our players regularly attended these services. This was their way of preparing spiritually for the upcoming game. Someone once said, "There are no atheists in the foxholes." There are few before football games, as well.

Bob Devaney implemented the tradition of asking the players to "take a knee" before going out on the field prior to the start of a game, and I continued that practice. This short period of time provided an opportunity for players to meditate on their upcoming performance, as well as on their relationship to God. Although I am sure that many of them got down on their knees out of habit, I think that most genuinely entered into an attitude of prayer at that time. Each player grabbed the hand of a teammate kneeling next to him. During that moment, there was a strong sense of unity and purpose among those present.

Following each game, the first thing we did upon coming off the field was to again take a knee for a moment of silent prayer. This time gave everyone a chance to calm down and focus their thoughts. Whether we had just enjoyed a win or suffered a loss, "taking a knee" provided a stabilizing moment of reflection.

After professional and collegiate football games, it has become common for players and coaches from both teams to kneel together near the 50-yard line and have a short prayer. One positive aspect of this public prayer is the display of solidarity and brotherhood between players on opposing teams. Many football fans fail to realize that even with the violence and intensity of the game, there is still love and respect among the young men on both sides.

There are many people who object to public displays of religion. In an article published in the *Omaha World Herald* in October of 1998, David Moshman, a University of Nebraska professor and a member of the ACLU, expressed concern that the University of Nebraska's football program violated the U.S. Constitution's principle of the separation of church and state. On the other hand, in the same article, running back Dan Alexander described faith as the backbone of our football program. Dan expressed his belief that the spiritual commitment of many of the coaches was contagious and contributed to a 100 percent work ethic in practice. He said, "That's what has made this program great—the force behind the winning." In the same newspaper article, defensive end Aaron Wills attributed overcoming drug and alcohol problems, which had threatened his football career, his education, and his life, to a spiritual turnaround aided by Receivers Coach Ron Brown. Many players felt they benefited from the spiritual environment of the team. They also appreciated no one being pressured to accept any belief or religious practice they were uncomfortable with.

Tom Landry often said he could not recall changing the character of even one of his players in all of his years as coach of the Dallas Cowboys. By the time a player reached the Cowboys he was at least 22 years old, and Tom felt that the player's character was fully developed by that time. He said that he did see some dramatic changes in the lives of a few players, but those changes were the result of the player's responding to God's working in their lives, not something he or his coaches did.

Players entering a college football program are younger than those in professional football. Therefore, we saw some character improvement in our athletes attributable to their college environment. However, even by age 18, their basic character had been molded and dramatic change was rare.

I was concerned about the long-term well-being of our players. The most challenging cases were those who had been raised well, had been exposed to good values, and appeared to be grounded in faith, yet deliberately turned their backs on what they knew God would have them be. It was disheartening to see a player embarked on a self-destructive course sure to cause pain to those who cared about him. Although some players didn't change, many did. If such a turnaround occurred, it was almost always because the player entered into a vital relationship with God.

It is human instinct to put ourselves first. This innate tendency is what some refer to as "original sin." My experience, and that of others, has been that self-centeredness isn't very satisfying long term. As Irving Fryar, a former Nebraska and NFL player, said at one point, he got "sick and tired of being sick and tired." Irving had been caught up in the drug scene early in his NFL career, was often angry, and, on one self-destructive occasion, left a game at halftime and ran his car into a tree at high speed. Like several of our players, Irving came to the place where he could not find peace in possessions or football accomplishments.

When he began to serve God rather than his own interests, everything in Irving's life seemed to fit together. Though Irving led a rather troubled existence for several years, he eventually "hit bottom," had a spiritual conversion, and became an ordained minister. Irving and many other former Nebraska players became almost totally different people when they allowed God to take control of their lives.

I don't believe God takes sides. Prayers of players on one side of the field don't take precedence over the prayers of those on the other side of the field when a last-second, game-deciding field goal is attempted. Cynical individuals assume that religious practices surrounding athletics are merely superstition or good-luck charms. Some religious practices are of this nature; however, over time I could see a genuine spiritual growth among many of our players that had the stamp of authenticity.

If God is the author of love, unity, wisdom, courage, and self-sacrifice, it seems foolish to factor Him out of life's equation. The qualities that make human experience all that it can possibly be emanate from Him.

Honoring God was the most logical and worthwhile goal. When I honored Him with the way that I coached, recruited, dealt with my family, and dispensed material resources, things seemed to be in sync and life had purpose and meaning. When I did not honor Him, life seemed to be out of focus. It was easy to get so caught up in trying to win games that my relationship with God (and my family, as well) did not have proper priority. It was not that God wasn't important to me, He just got crowded out by the demands of coaching.

I don't want to appear sanctimonious. There were times when I failed to be the person my faith called me to be. I am reminded of a prayer that an elderly nursing home resident sent to me. It goes like this:

> Dear Lord, so far today, God, I've done all right. I haven't gossiped, haven't lost my temper, haven't been greedy, grumpy, nasty, selfish, or overindulgent. I am very thankful for that, but in a few minutes, God, I'm going to get out of bed and from then on I am probably going to need a lot more help. Amen.

From my teenage years on through my mid-twenties, athletics often was preeminent among my priorities. When I was no longer an athlete, my pursuit of graduate degrees occupied most of my time and energies. From age 28 through 35, my major focus was seeking a head football coaching position. After becoming a head coach at age 35, winning football games was often foremost in my life. As I grew older and underwent open heart surgery, I occasionally placed financial security at the top of my list of priorities.

Jesus indicated that "saving" one's life through the pursuit of possessions, security, power, and pleasure would ultimately cause us to lose our lives. The things we put first in our lives are often dead ends and cause us to lose our lives in a spiritual sense. On the other hand, serving and honoring God leads to life. Even though my faith was very important from the time I committed my life to Christ at age 20, I still struggled with my priorities. I often honored self, career, and possessions more than I honored God and my family. "First place" in one's life is not dependent upon what is said, but rather on what occupies center stage in terms of time, talent, and resources. The amount of time I gave to football bordered on idolatry.

Jesus said, "I have come that you might have life, and have it more abundantly." The fullest, most meaningful way in which to experience life is to live in a relationship with God through the power and grace afforded us by Jesus. Being somewhat compulsive and having grown up in the world of athletics, where achievement is predicated on hard work, grace has been a difficult concept for me to grasp. The idea that a relationship with God is not achieved by effort and good works, but is freely given, seems too good to be true. As the reality of the depth and breadth of God's love impacts a person in the depths of that person's being, life begins to assume a different pattern. I have experienced grace as I have contemplated God's love as exemplified by Jesus' death on the cross. I also discern God's grace as I look back on events in my life such as my marriage to Nancy, the lives of my children, career decisions, and the many players and coaches I have interacted with. Often I was unaware of God's hand at many junctures along the way, but in retrospect I can see His grace.

Reggie White, an all-pro defensive lineman with the Green Bay Packers, recently said, "God honors those who honor Him."

Some might construe Reggie's quote to mean that if you are faithful, God will always give you what you want. My experience has been that God's ways are not our ways and many times honoring Him produces unexpected results. An example of this was the 1984 Orange Bowl. We lost to Miami 31–30 in one of the most memorable games ever played. I recall praying before the game that we might play in a way that would honor God. We attempted a two-point pass to win at the end of the game and failed on the conversion as a defensive back from Miami got a finger on the football and deflected it. We were probably no more than a half-inch away from victory and a national championship. However, God used that loss and failed two-point conversion to affect people in a surprising way. Some saw it as another botched attempt to win a national championship, and some saw quite another thing.

The way we played the game, coming back from a 17-point deficit and going for the win at the end instead of kicking the point and assuring a national championship, had a deep effect on people. They attached a spiritual significance to the failed two-point play that transcended the actual events of the game. They felt we played a game that honored God. It hurt to lose, but I still felt blessed to have participated in a game where players from both sides displayed great skill, courage, and unity.

Sometimes a catastrophic event can have a positive impact. The death of Brook Berringer in the spring of 1996 was a devastating loss. Brook was our starting quarterback most of the season, and we won the national championship following the 1994 season. His life was cut short by a plane crash at a time when he had everything going for him. He had graduated from college and was about to be drafted into the National Football League. Life was good, and then all of a sudden he was gone. Yet because of the way he lived his life and because of his faith and personal testimony, Brook's death had meaning. Our players saw firsthand how fragile and tenuous life is. They also saw the difference between living a life consistent with God's purpose, no matter how brief, and living a life that is without God and without ultimate meaning. Brook had recommitted his life to Christ several months before he died and was a powerful witness to those who knew him. Someone once said, "Live life in such a way that those who know you, but don't know God, will come to know God because they know you." Brook, through his life and his death, was allowed to show many people who God is.

A nucleus of spiritually committed athletes can have a major impact on a football team. Speaking in an ESPN interview at the January 1999 East-West Game, University of Tennessee captain Jeff Hall referred to the spiritual presence on the 1998 national championship football team. Jeff noted that Tennessee had graduated many key players the previous year, including their great quarterback, Payton Manning. However, the spiritual bond formed among the players had much to do with Tennessee's 13–0 record in 1998. Tennessee coach Phillip Fulmer commented on the outstanding unity he saw on his team. I am sure that the spiritual commitment of many of the players had something to do with the exceptional attitude.

I believe that players who truly are intent on honoring God with their lives and with their play make a difference. The spiritual atmosphere on our team, although not perfect, was generally conducive to mutual respect and self-sacrifice. It certainly enhanced the chemistry of our team.

I do not want to portray our football program as a monastic order. We certainly experienced challenges and conflicts. Some players tested us more than others; however, there was a love and concern on our team that was a great catalyst to team unity. Some of that love and concern could be traced to a very noticeable spiritual presence.

Trev Alberts, an All-American defensive end and first-round NFL draft choice following the 1993 season, mentioned the impact that David Seizys had on him. David wasn't big and did not have great speed. His strong desire to honor God with his play and his willingness to share that commitment were contagious. David had a significant impact on our team that greatly exceeded his physical talents. There have been many David Seizyses over the years who have served as the leaven that made the total program productive.

Amos Alonzo Stagg, one of the most respected football coaches of all time, said:

> You must love your boys to get the most out of them and do the most for them. I have worked with boys whom I haven't

admired, but have loved them just the same. Love has domi-
nated my coaching career, as I am sure it has and always will
that of many other coaches and teachers.

I think that the spirit of love that Stagg refers to was apparent
to our players and created a greater capacity for the players to
love others, as well.

◾ 3 ◾
Honesty

Truth has no special time of its own.
Its hour is now—always.
—Albert Schweitzer

The old adage "honesty is the best policy" has been severely tested in today's culture. Most Americans have been raised to believe that, long term, honesty will pay off. Intercollegiate athletics, however, has challenged this notion. On more than one occasion, schools have rapidly achieved athletic success through dishonest means.

During the 1970s and 1980s, there were times when we played teams who were not recruiting with the same scholarship that we offered. Illegal inducements were often extended to key recruits. There was always a temptation to adopt the philosophy "if you can't beat them, join them." Some coaches who were inherently honest did just that, rationalizing that they and their assistants would be fired if they didn't "fight fire with fire." This period of time was a true test of faith. I knew that God requires honesty and faithfulness—yet the temptation was there.

I recall recruiting an outstanding running back in Texas 15 years ago. With the approval of his high school coach and parents, this young man had verbally committed to play at Nebraska. He not only told our coaches that he was definitely coming to Nebraska, but he also informed the newspapers of his decision. As a coaching staff, we felt confident that his commitment was solid. A few days before the national letter of intent signing date, however, we received a call from the player's high school coach. The coach informed me that something "fishy" was going on and that I needed to see the player immediately. Someone in the community informed the coach that the young man's family had deposited $10,000 into a savings account; the family did not have that kind of money. The coach also noticed deterioration in the player's attitude, which led him to believe that something irregular was going on. Jerry Pettitbone, the Nebraska assistant who recruited the young man, and I flew to Texas, but we could not locate the player. His coach couldn't find him, and the player's parents claimed they did not know where he was. It was obvious he did not want to see us, and we suspected another school was involved with his disappearance. Not surprisingly, two days later, the young man signed with a school other than Nebraska.

A few years later, that same school was charged with numerous violations. One of the violations indicated that an alumnus had flown to see the player in question on his private plane. As the plane sat on the tarmac, the wealthy alumnus invited the player to sit in the back of his jet and drew up an agreement on a legal pad outlining $60,000 worth of benefits. Needless to say, we lost the player. The young man turned out to be an outstanding college player and went on to perform well in the National Football League. His college team improved from being a doormat to being a good team, but was never of championship caliber. It wasn't long before the team was placed on probation with sanctions. The NCAA penalties eliminated television and bowl appearances and also reduced scholarship numbers. The sanctions precipitated a downward spiral, leaving the team in worse shape than ever.

Sacrificing honesty for recruiting advantages was not uncommon in college football. There was a time during the 1980s when most schools in the Southwest Conference were on probation. The most striking case involved SMU. Although SMU had previously been placed on probation for recruiting violations, key boosters decided to continue making illegal payments to players. Since these athletes had been promised money before SMU was put on probation, the boosters rationalized their actions as being the "honorable" thing to do, as they did not want to break a promise.

The chairman of the SMU board of regents, Bill Clements, was involved in the decision to continue providing extra benefits to the players. At that time, he was running for governor and was subsequently elected governor of Texas. Since SMU had been on probation and then committed a second series of serious violations, their program received the "sudden death" penalty in 1985 and was shut down. This penalty prevented SMU from playing football for two years and completely dismembered a once-proud football organization. The ruling was historic, as it demonstrated that persistent, deliberate patterns of cheating would no longer be tolerated.

The widespread cheating and subsequent sanctions among Southwest Conference schools led to a significant number of Texas high school players choosing to attend schools outside the state of Texas. This exodus was prompted by many Southwest Conference schools' being placed on probation and unable to participate in bowl games or televised games. Forces were set in motion that, at least in part, ultimately resulted in the Southwest Conference dissolving after the 1995 season.

Following the 1985 penalty levied against SMU, things began to change. While some cheating still occurred, coaches began to realize that the NCAA was serious. It was not long before the flagrant cheating involving offers of cash, cars, clothing, and travel disappeared. Since the late 1980s, I have not been aware of a single player who I felt chose a school because of the promise of illegal inducements. This general observation relates only to Division I football. I don't know what has occurred in other sports, and there may have been cheating in football of which I was unaware. There is no question, however, that the level of honesty of football coaches today is much better than at any time in my coaching experience.

Recruiting, however, did not suddenly become entirely ethical. Much of the blatant and sensational cheating disappeared, but a good deal of subtle dishonesty still persists. Coaches frequently promise playing time. It is not unusual for high school seniors to be guaranteed a certain amount of playing time, or even a starting position as a college freshman. Promising playing time to high school seniors is fundamentally dishonest and is unfair to players who are already on the team. Playing time and starting positions should be earned on the playing field, not given away as recruiting inducements.

Several years ago we were recruiting a quarterback who was sure to come to Nebraska. His high school coach was a Nebraska fan and visited our coaching staff each spring. The offense the player's high school ran was the University of Nebraska offense, right down to the numbering system. The player had shown great interest in Nebraska for two years. Unexpectedly, we lost the young man to another school. The coach who recruited him to the rival school told me that he had promised the quarterback playing time as a true freshman and explained this was the reason the young man had chosen his school over Nebraska. The coach seemed proud of his accomplishment. While it was not a violation of NCAA rules to promise playing time to the young man, it was not ethical. Playing time should be based on merit. To make matters worse, promises of playing time are often not kept.

Another frequent recruiting ploy is to promise changing an offensive or defensive system to suit an individual recruit. A passing team often has trouble recruiting a great high school running back. Running backs usually want to attend colleges that run the ball most of the time. It is not unusual for coaches from a passing school to tell a running back that they are planning to change their offense. If the young man attends their school, they promise to alter the entire offensive system, abandon the passing game, and feature the recruited running back. The same scenario applies to a quarterback who is interested in throwing the ball 30 or 40 times a game. If a school recruiting him is not known for a passing attack, the coaches may promise to change their offensive philosophy and throw the football to accommodate the quarterback. Occasionally, defensive coaches will promise to change their defensive approach to appeal to the preferences of a great defensive recruit.

Most of the time, despite the promises, these schools have no intention of altering their strategies. Coaches are usually committed to a particular style of play and do not change. The high school recruit, once he is on the college campus, usually discovers that coaches don't change their philosophy for one recruit.

Sometimes a player will indicate his desire to pursue a particular academic major. Although the school recruiting him may not offer that major, coaches tell the recruit that they have a major almost identical to the course of study the player desires. I recall recruiting a young man from Oklahoma a few years ago named Spencer Tillman. Spencer indicated that he was interested in petroleum engineering, a major not offered at Nebraska. As

I visited with Spencer, I realized he was firmly set on making petroleum engineering his life's work. It hurt to do so, but I advised Spencer against attending Nebraska because we could not help him. Eventually, he went to the University of Oklahoma and played very well against us for four years. If we had convinced Spencer to come to Nebraska using the pretense of a course of study similar to petroleum engineering, we would have had a very disillusioned young man on our hands. A player who is recruited under false pretenses, no matter how talented, will usually not work out, as he resents being misled.

It is not unusual for a high school recruit to be told that attending a particular school will assure him of being a high draft pick in the National Football League. If the college coaches making such promises have previously coached in the NFL, these assurances gain credibility. Obviously, no high school senior can realistically be projected as a high draft choice in professional football. I was always intrigued when players chose a college based on where they would be drafted in the NFL before they had even played a down of college football.

There are times when coaches conceal recruiting commitments. Prospective recruits usually want to know what other players have committed to attend a school, particularly those who play the same position. In the 1970s, we recruited a young man who had previously committed to the University of Alabama. He had understood that he would be one of only two running backs to be recruited that year. When Alabama's recruiting list was released to the newspaper, however, there were eight running backs committed to Alabama. Since he had not yet signed a letter of intent, and being concerned about the large number of running backs, the young man contacted us and came to Nebraska. He started at Nebraska for three years and later played for the Miami Dolphins in the NFL. Bear Bryant, the legendary Alabama coach, didn't forget the episode. He brought it up as we talked before our 1977 game with Alabama in Lincoln. He was not happy about losing a great running back from the state of Alabama.

During the recruiting season, a similar scenario occurs many times. The recruit is often unaware of how much competition he has at his position until after the letter of intent has been signed. In August, many young men show up on their college campuses only to find that more players were recruited for their position than they were led to believe. This type of dishonesty can bring about feelings of resentment and betrayal among players before they even begin their college careers.

College coaches are very tempted to make it seem quick and easy for a high school player to play immediately. Realistically, however, it is seldom quick or easy for a freshman to play. There are many players in every program who have outstanding talent. Players who are given the impression that they will have little competition for a starting job usually receive a rude awakening on the first day of practice.

Sometimes a recruiting visit to a campus is a lesson in deceit. In accordance with NCAA rules, each high school senior is allowed five expense-paid "official" visits. During these visits, they can be on the college campus for 48 hours. However, the time spent on campus is often not a true representation of what the player will encounter when he attends school. Some universities have a young woman meet the player upon his arrival at the airport and take him to a series of parties. The player may not see the coaching staff until the next day. I have had recruits explain that on some visits, they would not see the school, the athletic department, or the academic facilities until the morning of the third and final day of their visit. Nearly their whole weekend was spent going to parties.

Such recruiting visits leave prospects with a distorted image of major college athletics. Attending a university as a student-athlete does not leave a great deal of time for socializing. Athletes are required to spend time in study halls, classes, meetings with coaches, the weight room, and on the practice field. If one expects to stay on track toward accomplishing his or her goals, social life is only a minor part of the experience. However, the high school senior, as he goes through the recruiting process, is often not exposed to the harsh realities of being a student-athlete.

Since we can't offer mountains, beaches, or a vibrant social life in Lincoln, Nebraska, we maximized the resources and advantages we could offer. When a player visited our campus, we made sure that he got a realistic idea of what he would be required to do and where he would spend most of his time. The academic counselors provided each recruit with an example of the class schedule he would have if he enrolled at Nebraska the next fall. He participated in a comprehensive tour that took the better part of one day. During this time, the recruit would tour the academic facilities and visit with a faculty member in his field of study, as well as meet with the academic support staff. Each young man had extensive sessions with strength coaches, athletic trainers, equipment personnel, assistant coaches, and the head coach. In addition, we made sure he saw our athletic facilities, had a campus tour, got acquainted with the city, and talked with a number of current players. The weekend was designed to provide the player with an accurate picture of what life as a student-athlete is like at Nebraska. The visit was not flashy—it was based on the realities of major-college athletics.

This recruiting approach sometimes backfired. If a player was primarily interested in parties and social life, he often chose a school that emphasized social activities in the recruitment process. It was the young men who were primarily focused on educational goals and a solid football career that we had a good chance to recruit. Losing some recruits proved beneficial. I recall two young men from Mississippi whom we recruited. They were very interested in Nebraska and had given us a preliminary indication that they wanted to play in our program. However, they stayed out very late the first night of their visit and slept most of the next day—missing the appointments we had set up for them. Needless to say, we informed them that we were no longer recruiting them.

A player who chose to attend Nebraska with the assumption that his social life would overshadow his academic achievement and his football career was going to be disappointed. His priorities would be all wrong. He would likely become disillusioned and leave, no matter how talented he was.

It was important that team members hosting a recruit had a chance to provide feedback and share their impression of the young man. Occasionally, the host discouraged us from further recruiting a player because of behavior he observed. We listened carefully to such warnings, as our players often saw a side of the recruit in informal settings of which the coaches were unaware.

Whenever possible, we encouraged the parents of a recruit to accompany him on his visit. While the glamour and the glitz of other programs might be more appealing to an 18-year-old player, we felt that what we had to offer was appealing to adults. Therefore, we were often very successful in recruiting players who had their families accompany them. Parents usually looked for substance and stability, even if their sons were more impressed by entertainment and transitory factors. In the long run, these parents knew, substance would be more important than social life.

As a coaching staff, we made sure each recruit was aware of his competition if he chose to play at Nebraska. We did not have secrets concerning the depth chart a recruit would encounter at his position. Although we lost some players in the process, those who chose Nebraska did so for the right reasons and most of them successfully completed their college career with us. We certainly were not perfect, and I am sure that on occasion a player may have felt he was not given all of the facts concerning Nebraska. However, our recruiting policy was intended to be as straightforward and honest as possible. We believed this philosophy not only reflected integrity but also benefited the future of the program.

Our recruiting classes were seldom highly rated by the experts; however, we placed little value on such assessments. In fact, we generally performed on the field at a much higher level than our perceived recruiting success would indicate. I attribute this phenomenon partially to the fact that we recruited young men who fit our program well and truly desired to play at Nebraska. These players usually remained true to their commitment to complete their playing career at Nebraska. At many schools, it was not unusual for highly recruited players to transfer because the expectations created by their recruiting visit did not match reality once they enrolled in school.

Honesty was not only important during recruiting, it was essential once the player was in the program. The assistant coaches met with each player in a formal interview at least twice a year, and the head coach met with each player at least once. During these individual meetings, the coaches provided the player with an honest assessment of where he stood. They discussed performance strengths and weaknesses, chances of playing, and attitudinal factors impacting the team. These meetings also gave the player an opportunity to express his views and concerns. Scheduling these formal interviews forced the players and coaches to sit down and deal with key issues in an honest, straightforward, and systematic manner. Problems often develop when players do not have an accurate understanding of how they fit into the larger picture.

We once had a defensive back from Los Angeles who believed he deserved a starting position. In reality, he was not only not a first-team player, but he was third team at best. He had some talent but would lose his poise in a game and play very erratically. The discrepancy between the player's perception of his talent and that of the coaches was amazing. As I discussed the situation with the player, it became obvious that his views were so out of touch with reality that there was no hope of reconciling our differences. The player eventually transferred to another school and had a similar experience. Eventually, this player realized that we had treated him fairly, and he loyally supports Nebraska today.

Pat Riley, professional basketball coach, recognized the importance of honesty in dealing with players when he said, "A coach must keep everyone on the team in touch with present realities— knowing where they stand, knowing where they're falling short of their potential—and knowing it openly and fairly."

If a player was told that he was going to play in a game, it was imperative that we followed through on the promise. However, game situations are unpredictable and such promises can be difficult to keep. During the early part of the 1997 season, we were trying to get experience for our number-two quarterback, Frankie London. If our number-one quarterback, Scott Frost, were to be injured and out for a significant period of time, we wanted Frankie to feel confident and prepared to step in. Prior to the Central Florida game, we told both young men that Frankie would enter the game and play a series of downs in the second quarter. We anticipated having a lead by that point in the game but were actually behind. Despite trailing in the second quarter, we wanted to keep our word and put Frankie in the game. He immediately led our team on a touchdown drive.

This performance created a quarterback controversy. Many fans thought we pulled Scott Frost for playing poorly and should have kept Frankie in the game. This was not the case at all, however. We followed the initial script, played Frankie the prescribed amount of time, and put Scott back into the game. Scott was booed by a number of fans as he reentered the game. The whole episode was not only embarrassing to Scott, it was somewhat disruptive to the team and did not go as our coaching staff had envisioned. Despite the controversy, it was important that our actions were consistent with our words. If we had not played Frankie as we said we would, some of Frankie's trust in us would have been broken and both quarterbacks would have drawn the conclusion that we would not keep our word. Scott Frost went on to have a great senior season, but the situation in the Central Florida game proved to be unsettling for a short time.

Inconsistency between actions and words exists on all levels of competition. A former Nebraska player who went on to the National Football League recalled being described by the coaches on the professional team as their "best running back," and was informed that they had big plans for him. When he went to practice, however, he spent most of his time on the sidelines. He was given very little practice repetition and was treated as a third-team running back. The confusion that resulted from the conflicting statements and actions of the coaching staff led him to eventually quit the team. I am confident this young man could have been a valuable contributor to the organization if the coaches had simply leveled with him about his role on the team from the beginning. If he had been told up front that he was a backup player, he would have been able to handle his lack of practice time. Instead, he became so frustrated by the lack of honesty that his career ended long before it should have.

When one person lies to another, trust is destroyed. From that point on, it is difficult to know when the person who lied is being honest. Over time, I've had players who lied to me. Although I continued to coach them and care about them, I never again had the same level of trust in those players as I did with the players who were honest with me. I always respected and trusted a player who owned up to his mistakes, no matter how bad they were.

In his book *People of the Lie,* Dr. Scott Peck refers to lying as a crime against others. He explains that although crimes can be of greater and lesser magnitudes, it is a mistake to think of them as a matter of degree. "Under certain circumstances, dishonest behavior may be more excusable, but the fact remains that they are all lies and betrayals." Our culture is far down the slippery slope of relativism. In many situations, lying is not only common, it is expected. As we accept and excuse dishonesty as a nation, we are undermining the foundation of our society. Every culture is held together by the assumption of a certain level of honesty. Once those assumptions are no longer valid, the wheels start to come off.

Honesty was mentioned consistently in our meetings as a major part of our team culture. It was important for players to be honest with me and the other coaches, but it was even more important that the coaches and I were honest with the players. When a player felt deceived by the coaches, his trust and confidence in the coaching staff was seriously shaken. Although I'm sure there may have been players who felt they were lied to or misled by the coaching staff, I hope such an occurrence was rare. The policy established for the coaching staff was to be honest with each player at all times.

It was every bit as important for a coach to have accurate feedback concerning his status and performance as it was for a player to have that information. I met at least once a year with each assistant and graduate assistant coach. During these meetings, I provided an honest assessment of how I felt they were doing. We would discuss strengths and areas that needed to be improved, as well as problems they had with me or the players. The more honest and frank these meetings were, the more productive we became as a coaching staff.

When two people are face-to-face, there is always a temptation to sugarcoat bad news or exaggerate the good qualities that a person displays. Confrontation is never comfortable. However, only when the coach has accurate information can he plan for the future and make necessary changes in his coaching. Dealing with shortcomings and problem areas early, although uncomfortable at the time, benefits everyone in the long run. I had very few coaches who did not adjust their coaching style when asked to do so. Honest communication was an important part of meaningful change.

It was equally important that I received accurate feedback from the coaches and players regarding my performance. Since they were under my supervision, it was often difficult for them to express concerns and criticisms of how I was doing. Sometimes I had to "read between the lines" to discover that certain actions or behaviors were perceived as disappointing or inappropriate. One of the problems associated with being at the top of an organization is limited, often inaccurate feedback from those one super-vises. This can lead to a distorted view of one's own importance and effectiveness. The coach, administrator, or leader who sur-rounds himself with people who shower him with accolades to build up his ego is on a fast track toward losing touch with reality.

I recall an instance when one of my coaches called me late one night and informed me he was very disappointed that I had hired a new coach at a higher salary than he was receiving. He assumed that new coaches always started at the bottom of the salary scale. I explained that hiring a new coach who was already making a good salary necessitated my giving the coach at least a slight raise in order to get him to come to Nebraska. Sometimes the new coach would be paid more than coaches already on the staff because of his previous salary. The assistant who called me eventually understood the situation, and we continued to have a good relationship. Even though the phone call was confronta-tional and unpleasant, I was glad he felt comfortable in calling me and letting me know how he felt. If he had not called, his concern would have festered and I would not have known that a problem even existed. Being out of touch with things as they really are, good or bad, is certain to result in ineffective manage-ment. As John Madden, former Oakland Raiders coach, describes, "You have to hear things you really don't want to hear; you must look at things you really don't want to see."

Currently, there is an almost cavalier disregard for truth in politics, business, athletics, and even within families. People go to great lengths to either deceive or manipulate facts to make things appear to be something other than what they really are. Our unwillingness to state things plainly and with veracity has led to much cynicism and mistrust. In his letter to the Philippi-ans, the apostle Paul points out the importance of honesty and how it elevates thought and performance. "Finally, brothers, whatever is true, whatever is noble, whatever is right, whatever is pure, whatever is lovely, whatever is admirable—if anything is excellent or praiseworthy—meditate on these things."

Honesty is necessary in holding things together. Honest rela-tionships are built on a common sense of trust and confidence among the individuals involved. Trust and confidence in each other was an important part of our team chemistry.

> *The staff must truly stick together during tough times. . . .*
> *No offense should be viewed more seriously than disloyalty.*
> **—Bill Walsh, former San Francisco 49ers coach**

Loyalty binds people together and causes them to put others ahead of personal ambition. In John 6:66–68, we see the importance of loyalty to Jesus and his disciples: "From this time many of his disciples turned back and no longer followed Him. 'You do not want to leave too, do you?' Jesus asked the twelve. Simon Peter answered Him, 'Lord, to whom shall we go? You have the words of eternal life.'" Without the loyalty of a handful of followers, Jesus' mission would have been severely handicapped.

One of the great memories I have of my father was the loyalty and devotion he showed toward my mother. My mother had a severe stroke at age 72, which rendered her speechless and partially paralyzed. Despite health problems associated with his heart disease, my father cared for and assisted her, attending to her needs. The effort expended in getting her in and out of a wheelchair and in and out of bed hastened his own death four years later. He stood by her, however, and did everything he could to make her comfortable.

Loyalty became a major issue at the conclusion of my senior year in high school. I had had some success as a high school athlete and was offered football scholarships to several universities. I also was offered basketball scholarships by several schools.

However, since age ten, I had lived across the street from Hastings College, a small liberal arts school located in my hometown, Hastings, Nebraska. As I grew up, I spent every spare moment at the college football field or basketball gymnasium. Tom

McLaughlin, the football and track coach, had developed a good relationship with me. I liked Tom and trusted him. My father, grandfather, and two uncles had played football at Hastings College, so I heard many stories about past athletic teams. I knew every player, every coach, watched every athletic contest, and grew up with a strong loyalty to Hastings College.

I considered several schools, but when decision time came, I found that my allegiance to Hastings College was stronger than the attraction of playing football or basketball at a major university. I enrolled at Hastings with no scholarship aid and paid my way through school for the next four years. Some of my friends were shocked by my decision, and the coaches at Division I schools were very surprised. I even surprised myself when I found that I could not turn my back on the school that had meant so much to me during my formative years.

Staying with people and institutions who were somehow influential and important to me has remained a persistent pattern. I can honestly say that I have not regretted any decision I have made based on loyalty.

As I think back over 36 years of involvement with Nebraska football, I realize that loyalty has been a dominant factor throughout that period of time. On April 25, 1998, my "retirement" banquet, involving 700 players and coaches who had been part of Nebraska football since 1962, was held at the Bob Devaney Sports Center on the University of Nebraska campus. It was surprising that so many former players and coaches attended, and it seemed that there was a very strong common bond among all of those who were present. Their devotion and loyalty to the University of Nebraska, and the football program in particular, were very apparent. There was a powerful bond that drew us together; the feeling was so strong that it was almost tangible. This common bond was not a random event, but rather came directly from a strong sense of loyalty instilled by Bob Devaney, who was the head football coach at the University of Nebraska from 1962 through the 1972 season and continued as athletic director until 1992.

Bob was one of those "old school" coaches who believed that if you played for him or coached for him, you were one of his. He would always take time to show that he remembered you, cared about you, and was interested in what you were doing. He had a knack for making people feel at ease. Through his sense of humor and personal charisma, he created a strong sense of devotion among his players. Bob had a temper and at times could be fairly volatile, but these periods of anger never lasted long. He was quick to forgive and always made the object of his wrath feel accepted and comfortable within a short period of time.

Bob stood behind his players and coaches through thick and thin. In 1967 and 1968, Nebraska had "bad" years—both ending 6–4, the only two seasons in 37 years (1962–98) in which Nebraska did not go to a bowl game. The 1968 season ended with a 47–0 thumping by Oklahoma in Norman, Oklahoma. Nebraska fans were not happy, and there was a good deal of grumbling.

It is fairly common when things are not going well for a team for the head coach to fire either the offensive assistants or the defensive staff. This decision deflects blame and responsibility from the head coach. The wolves want sacrificial lambs when you lose.

Bob Devaney had pressure to get rid of some coaches after the second 6–4 season, but he insisted that either the whole staff would go or no one would go. He refused to blame any assistant or player. He maintained a steady resolve and was supportive of all of those he worked with. Everyone on Bob's staff felt needed and appreciated. This loyalty was rewarded by two national championship seasons, in 1970 and 1971. Somehow our coaches must have gotten a lot smarter in only two years, as there was suddenly no longer any talk of getting rid of coaches.

This attitude of "we're all in this together" has persisted to the present day. Each coach on Bob's staff and my staff knew that he would not become a scapegoat if things got tough. I have always believed that if one area of a football team is not performing well, it is the head coach's responsibility to see that the necessary adjustments are made to produce the desired performance. Most assistant coaches are willing to learn, and I believe this is true for people in all kinds of jobs. If they won't follow instructions or make an effort to improve, then a change may be required. It was my job as head coach to make sure people knew what was expected of them and to recommend areas for improvement. In my 25 years as a head coach, I dismissed only two coaches. Had I been more specific concerning what I expected earlier in those coaches' careers at Nebraska, both might have been saved.

Our coaching staff has been remarkably stable. The average tenure of our assistant coaches is 14 years, compared to an NCAA Division I average of about three years. Several of the assistant coaches who were there at or near the beginning of my career as head coach were with me at the end and still remain at Nebraska. Many of our coaches have had opportunities to move on in the coaching profession, at either the college or the professional level. These opportunities usually promised higher salaries and occasionally entailed coordinator or head coaching positions. But our coaches have chosen to stay at Nebraska primarily because of their loyalty to the program.

I can't emphasize enough how important staff continuity has been to the success of our program. When a coach leaves a staff, it is usually at the end of the football season—and right in the middle of the recruiting season. When the assistant coach who is recruiting a young man leaves a university, the athlete loses his most important contact with that school. Unless the player has no other options available, it is very unusual to have the player eventually sign with the school from which the assistant left. Since schools lose approximately three out of nine football assistants in an average year, about one-third of those schools' recruiting capacity is seriously impaired. We averaged losing only one assistant every two or three years, so our recruiting consistency was excellent.

The benefits of staff continuity extend beyond recruiting. We had to spend very little time "coaching the coaches." When a new coach joins the staff, he must learn terminology, personnel, and a whole new culture. Since our coaches were together for so long, we seldom had to slow the learning process so new coaches could be brought up to speed.

Even though I was never a particularly hot commodity in the coaching profession, there were a few opportunities to go into professional football or to other major universities for a higher salary. But any coaching offer that was of interest to me became a staff decision, rather than a personal decision. The only offer I took seriously was from the University of Colorado following my sixth year as head coach. We had trouble beating Oklahoma early in my career, losing the first five times we played. We finally won in 1978, 17–14, over a top-ranked Oklahoma team. We were so emotionally spent that we lost to Missouri the next week and were told we had to play Oklahoma again in the Orange Bowl. Playing Oklahoma a second time in only six weeks after finally beating them was a hard thing to swallow. In the rematch, we outgained Oklahoma in total yardage but lost, 31–24.

I was discouraged and frustrated. Some fans had been fairly negative, as we hadn't been as dominant as they had hoped. So, when the Colorado job was offered, I talked the situation over with my coaching staff. We agreed that Colorado appeared to be an easier recruiting situation, and the coaches shared some of my disappointment concerning fan reaction. So it was decided that I would go to Boulder and take a look. When my wife, Nancy, and I made the trip, I thought that we would take the job. The facilities were good and the location was as nice as we had thought, yet on the return trip to Lincoln, I thought about how I would break the news to the Nebraska players that I was leaving. The more I tried to construct that speech in my mind, the more I realized I couldn't make it. I had told those players that Nebraska was the best place for them, and I didn't know how I could now tell them that someplace else was better for me and the coaches. I sat down with the staff and told them I couldn't leave, and I never took a serious look at another job.

Even when I was still considering the move, however, the staff knew that we were a package. If I went, all those who wanted to go could join me. It is not uncommon for a head coach to take a job and leave most of his previous staff stranded. If the assistants don't go with the head coach, the new head coach coming in often doesn't hire them either. But it's important to realize that the consequences of your actions often reach far beyond your personal interests. Each year many assistant coaches and their families are abandoned by a head coach who has left for a situation that will benefit him personally.

The loyalty issue was put to the test during the 1995 season to a degree that I had not previously experienced. Just before the season began, Riley Washington, a third-team wingback, was accused of attempted murder in the shooting of an individual at a Quick Stop parking lot. Not long after that incident, Lawrence

Phillips, our starting I-back, was charged with assaulting a former girlfriend. Then Damon Benning, our second-team I-back, was charged with assault. The media really zoomed in on us. They publicized troubles that Christian Peter, one of our defensive tackles, had had three years previously. For good measure, they also mentioned pending charges against cornerback Tyrone Williams, who had been cited two years earlier.

I visited with Riley Washington almost daily over the 13 days that he sat in a jail cell prior to his release on bond. At first, I didn't know what to think. The charges authorities had brought against Riley were immediate and extremely serious. Yet Riley looked me right in the eye and said he was innocent. I had not known Riley to lie to me before. As I visited with him, he continued to express his innocence in a way that led me to believe that he was telling the truth. His attorneys at the public defender's office were able to gain information that substantiated Riley's claim of innocence. They presented their findings to me, Athletic Director Bill Byrne, University of Nebraska–Lincoln Chancellor Joan Leitzel, faculty representative Jim O'Hanlon, and Vice Chancellor for Student Affairs Jim Griessen. Those present agreed that it appeared Riley had been wrongly accused. I was given the green light to go ahead and play Riley during the season. This decision led to a good deal of negative press. The perception was that Riley was being allowed to play merely to help us win football games, despite having been charged with a serious crime. Since Riley was not a starter or key player, it seemed to me that the argument was rather hollow.

I doubt that there were more than a handful of people in the state of Nebraska who believed in Riley's innocence. The publicity surrounding the initial charges against him was so one-sided that most people's minds were made up before he was given his day in court.

Standing by Riley in the face of so much public condemnation was unpleasant. I believed that we had done our homework on the specifics of the case, however, and I believed in Riley. I realized that the university, the football program, and I would all come under increased criticism and derision if the facts as we understood them did not bear out.

Riley played sparingly during the last three-fourths of the season. He went to class, went to practice, and then went to his room. The court case dragged on over the next year and a half. He became more and more despondent, and at times seemed to despair of ever having his name cleared. There were many delays in the trial. The attorneys from the public defenders' office were anxious to try the case, as they were confident that Riley was innocent. Finally, more than a year and a half following the initial charges, Riley was absolved of any blame by a jury that deliberated only a very brief time.

Riley eventually decided to quit football, and, after a short period of time on the track team in the spring of 1996, left athletics for good. My assessment of the situation was that Riley's discouragement reached the point where he no longer had the energy or will to compete in athletics. At one time he was considered a top prospect for the Olympic Games as a sprinter. He also had the potential, because of his great speed, to be a receiver in the National Football League. To his credit, Riley did get his degree in four years and was eventually able to get a job.

I felt bad for Riley's mother, who lived in San Diego. Early in the legal process, she asked me to look after Riley, since she was so far away. She also told me that she had lost her job as a result of the negative publicity. It had been reported in San Diego that Riley had murdered someone and was a gang member. Riley's name had also been removed from the San Diego Hall of Champions. She wrote me as follows in February 1997, after I sent her a newspaper article detailing Riley's being cleared by the jury:

Thank you so very much for standing by Riley, and thank you for the news article. You had to be searching in the sports section of the San Diego paper to find anything about the trial outcome. The t.v. station that ran the information for a week when it first happened declined my request to mention his acquittal over the air. I don't think many people realize how much of his past and his future Riley lost by this ordeal. Thank you again; also to your staff and Coach Brown for having faith in my son. May God greatly bless all of you!

It was disturbing to see what Riley and his family went through when it seemed clear that he was innocent. The prosecution's primary witness had previously been convicted of lying to police, left the state, would not appear at the trial, and changed his story, saying he did not see the shooter and had only assumed that Riley had shot him. A person who had privately boasted that he had done the shooting and whose clothing matched that of the shooter (Riley's didn't) was never charged. By remaining loyal to Riley, we at least did not compound the damage done to his reputation and career.

Damon Benning's case was similar to Riley's in that he was innocent, as well. Within two weeks of being charged, he was completely cleared, but the damage was done. His being exonerated was not given much attention by the national media.

There has been a lot of publicity about the Lawrence Phillips episode. Lawrence was charged with two misdemeanors involving the assault of a former girlfriend and was dismissed from the football team for six games. He did not start two games after rejoining the team late in the season. He started our final game, the Fiesta Bowl, in which we beat Florida for the national championship.

Upon hearing about the assault incident, I was certain that Lawrence should be permanently dismissed from the team. He had not followed my instructions and had violated team policy. After learning more about the circumstances surrounding the event, however, I was not so certain that this decision would be the proper course of action. Lawrence and the young woman in question had been dating but had a troubled relationship. I had warned Lawrence to stay away from the young woman and had told the young woman to contact me if Lawrence tried to make contact with her. If any contact occurred, it was understood that Lawrence would be dismissed from the team. Both parties agreed not to see each other.

Despite the agreement and warnings, Lawrence and the young woman continued to see each other, and Lawrence was led to believe that there was still a relationship between them. Lawrence violated my order to stay away from the young lady, and she, in turn, violated her promise to inform me if he did contact her.

When I first saw Lawrence after the incident, he was badly shaken and broke down in tears. For most people, this reaction would not be unusual given the severity of the circumstances; however, for Lawrence it was highly unusual to show any emotion, particularly sorrow. He had grown up on the streets and had learned to protect himself by putting up a wall of invincibility and anger to keep people at a distance. In visiting with Barbara Thomas, a counselor who worked with Lawrence since he was 12 at a group home in Los Angeles, I discovered that she had never seen him cry. She was surprised when I told her that Lawrence had broken down, as he had always been careful to avoid any display of vulnerability.

I was not particularly moved by the fact that Lawrence cried; however, behind the mask, I did see a scared, hurt, and vulnerable young man. The person I caught a glimpse of was much different from the outward persona that Lawrence showed the world. Lawrence was abandoned by his father during infancy, and he and his mother parted when he was quite young. He was on his own at age 11 and adopted a tough exterior to protect himself from further rejection. I realized that he did have a reachable heart and decided that allowing him the possibility of earning his way back onto the team was the best thing I could do to turn Lawrence around. One more rejection would only harden him and make him more difficult to reach.

My faith has led me to believe that no person is exempt from the pull of God or beyond redemption, including Lawrence. One of the last times I saw Lawrence I gave him a New Testament and explained that the only solution I saw would involve a spiritual commitment. He had been scarred by his past, labeled as unfit for society by the media, and would be a marked man wherever he went. A change from the inside was necessary, but only God and Lawrence could make that change.

Many claimed that the reason Lawrence was allowed to return to the team was merely to improve our chances to win. However, Ahman Green stepped in and become a very effective I-back throughout the season. Our talent and team chemistry was such that no one came close to beating us. We did not need Lawrence at any point to ensure victory.

Many people wanted Lawrence thrown off the team permanently as an example to those who might become involved in gender violence. A university official who talked to the witnesses involved in the alleged incident between Lawrence and his former girlfriend told me that he had found no evidence that

Lawrence hit the girl. Most media reports described the incident as a "brutal beating." Many accounts of Lawrence's behavior were either untrue or exaggerated. Our disciplining Lawrence in accordance with the facts, as described by witnesses, police reports, and the victim, was not well received.

Christian Peter was another player singled out by the media in 1995. He was charged with groping a young woman from behind in a crowded bar (which he denied doing), and had two other scrapes with the law that were minor. I lost patience with Christian's immaturity and informed him that if there was more trouble, we would dismiss him from the team permanently. During the rest of his career at Nebraska, Christian behaved well both on and off the field. He matured into a good leader and team captain. Yet his troubles three years previous were played up in the national press as if they had just happened. This was painful for Christian, his family, and the program. We continued to stand by Christian. He had been disciplined previously in accordance with team policy, had faithfully attended counseling sessions for alcohol abuse, and had done reasonably well academically.

Serious allegations were also lodged against Tyrone Williams, one of our cornerbacks. Two and a half years before the 1995 season, Tyrone had been accused of firing a small-caliber gun at the back end of an occupied automobile. Tyrone entered a plea of innocent. His attorneys disagreed with the severity of the charges against him and his case languished in court for several years. We had to make a decision as to whether or not we would eliminate him from the program. The charges had not been proven and the case would not come to trial for some time. Tyrone had no history of any legal or behavioral problems before or after that one incident. He had been drinking that evening and abstained from using alcohol following the incident. He had practically no parental support and was on his own. We suspended Tyrone from the team for a period of time because he admitted to the possession of a firearm. He rejoined the team after the suspension and was a model player for the rest of his career at Nebraska.

I received a letter from Tyrone's wife in 1997, thanking us for standing by Tyrone during those years and informing me that Tyrone was an outstanding father and husband. It was gratifying to see Tyrone do well after leaving Nebraska. He had married, had been part of the 1996 Green Bay Packers world championship football team, and had become a person with a strong spiritual commitment.

Reviewing the 1995 season and the accusations leveled at our players is painful. Even though two of the five players accused of wrongdoing were found innocent, and though the remaining three players did not do some of the things they were accused of, it still hurt to see the whole team dragged through this unpleasantness. The reason I discuss this difficult time here is that it has to do with loyalty.

Standing by the players and remaining loyal to them produced a great deal of criticism. However, in every case but one, it appears that the players' behavior after leaving Nebraska justified the trust and confidence we showed in them. When dealing with behavioral problems, it is hard to win every battle.

Pride can be a real stumbling block. I had been proud of the fact that we maintained an excellent win-loss record over many years but had been even more proud of the fact that we had tried to do things the right way, exhibiting a positive public image.

As the 1995 season progressed, this favorable image was stripped away. People in Nebraska viewed our team with mixed emotions. They were proud of our on-the-field accomplishments, but were somewhat dismayed at what was being said about us off the field. The national media was generally less kind. We were publicly ridiculed, and our image suffered greatly. This criticism was hard to accept. We had put as much effort into academic achievement and developing our players' character as we had in trying to win football games. The great majority of our players had acquitted themselves very well, yet much of what we stood for had been destroyed.

Examining the situation from a spiritual perspective, I realized that wanting public approval and praise was natural but also contained unhealthy elements of pride. I spent time reviewing the scriptures concerning trials and tribulations and also explored the events challenging us in my prayer life. There were no guidelines or written manuals that outlined a clear course of action. Eventually, personal instincts and a belief system had to be the foundation of decision making.

Gaining public approval was always important to me, but so

was keeping my decisions consistent with my faith. It gradually became obvious that I couldn't have both. Even though it was painful, I came to the conclusion that the most important thing was to show concern and love for the people I was responsible for and do what I felt was right in the light of my faith.

The one redeeming factor through all of this negative attention was that the players seemed to understand and accept what I chose to do and grew closer as a team. The closeness and focus engendered by the difficulties we had gone through together was reflected by a greater commitment and a higher level of play on the football field.

It has been my belief that if a player is recruited to Nebraska and places his confidence in us, the program, in return, owes it to that player to stand behind him even when things are not going well. This does not mean that players were never dismissed from the program. We dismissed two or three players a year. However, in every case, we did so according to team policy and also gave the player adequate chances to correct his behavior before final dismissal.

Many people do not understand that players are often far from home and, in many cases, the coach becomes much like a parent. As John Wooden explained, "I often told my players that, next to my own flesh and blood, they were the closest to me. They were my children. . . . I always tried to be fair and give each player the treatment he earned and deserved."

Through the turmoil of the 1995 season, our players stayed focused and committed. They knew that each player on the team was valued and would be supported. No one would be sacrificed on the altar of public opinion for the sake of appearances. The troubled 1995 season ended with an undefeated season and a national championship victory over unbeaten Florida in the Fiesta Bowl. I will always remember the unity and the commitment to excellence of that team. The more we were ridiculed by the national media, the closer and the more focused the team became. The team unity and chemistry was due in large part to the loyalty the players and coaches had toward each other.

Our success on the field in no way justified the fact that we had some players who did not acquit themselves well. We had a few players who had not behaved well in previous years, but we were not defending national champions with a good chance of repeating. The spotlight was on us, and we found that we were being held to a higher standard. The players and coaches became more proactive, trying to anticipate and discourage any source of trouble before problems started. I redoubled efforts to communicate to the players the importance of sound character and could point out graphically how damaging poor choices by a few could be to the whole team. We had not recruited players who had known character defects previously, and we now became even more vigilant regarding flaws of this nature as we evaluated new prospects.

Many Nebraska coaches came up through the ranks. Most started out as graduate assistants and then progressed to full-time coaches. When a vacancy on the coaching staff occurred, both Bob Devaney and I gave first consideration to people already associated with the program. Bob named me head coach in 1973 after I had been a graduate assistant and assistant for 11 years. Milt Tenopir, offensive line coach; Dan Young, offensive line and kicking coach; Turner Gill, quarterback coach; Craig Bohl, linebacker coach; and Frank Solich, now the head coach, all started at Nebraska as graduate assistants. Through patience, hard work, and loyalty, they became outstanding coaches.

It seems that many organizations are fearful of internal hiring. This is particularly true of institutions of higher learning, where there is often much concern about "inbreeding." This hiring process often results in poor personnel choices. It is very difficult to know about a person's character, work habits, and ability to relate to others simply by looking at a résumé or conducting an interview. In working with people for a period of years, you can know exactly what they can do and how they will react in pressure situations.

My observation has been that people from within an organization are much more apt to stay and work hard for that organization. They are more likely to be motivated by a desire to see the organization they have helped build do well than by a desire for personal gain. Bill Walsh, former San Francisco 49ers coach and executive, says, "The best way to maintain the continuity of an already winning profile, however, is to hire from within."

Loyalty demonstrated at the top often results in loyalty from within the ranks. At the end of the 1996 season, two key players,

Jason Peter and Grant Wistrom, were eligible to enter the NFL draft after completing their junior seasons. Both were quite likely first-round picks and would have been instant millionaires, yet both chose to come back for their senior years. In today's environment, it is rare for an underclassman who is a first-round pick to return for his final year of intercollegiate competition.

We finished the 1996 season 11–2 after going undefeated and winning national championships in 1994 and 1995. The 11–2 finish was not good enough for Jason and Grant. They wanted to win it all one more time, and they became great leaders as we prepared for the 1997 season. Grant and Jason led conditioning drills in January and February. They pushed their teammates during spring football and they drove those around them with unusual intensity during the summer. They played great football as the season unfolded, and we ended up 13–0 and tied with Michigan for the national championship. We would not have been able to have the year we had without them.

Many of our football coaches stayed on in the athletic department when their coaching days were over. It is sometimes hard to maintain the pace, particularly in recruiting, as the years go by. It is also very hard to get a job with another organization once a coach reaches his fifties and sixties. Nebraska took care of its people, and this was noticed by other coaching staffs. Many coaches wanted to join the Nebraska football staff because they observed a loyalty to former coaches that is uncommon at other schools.

Loyalty is not valued as much as it once was in our culture. In professional athletics, we see continual movement of players and coaches as they look for more pay, a better contract, and more security. Professional teams often move from city to city to pursue a better financial situation. College coaches have joined the parade of those seeking a higher bidder. Contracts are often not honored and promises to players are quickly forgotten. A well-known television personality indicated that this was "the American way" as she moved from one network to another for a higher salary. This lack of stability and loyalty is certainly wearing thin with many fans.

I am often concerned when I hear coaches and players say, "I have to do what's best for me and my family," as they leave their present team for a better deal. There is very little concern for their teammates, coaches, organizations, and fans, and these decisions to "jump ship" are often not right for them and their families in the long run, with the turmoil caused by moving around frequently outweighing certain financial benefits. There are times when career moves are warranted; however, such moves should be made for the right reasons. It seems that too few decisions are made in our culture out of a concern for the common good. Too often money and self-interest are the only factors given much weight. Loyalty has become an almost forgotten attribute.

Loyalty has served Nebraska football well. If people are shown sincere interest, support, and a willingness to sacrifice for them, this expression of loyalty will often be returned. Loyalty was one quality I encountered time and again, and it was that quality that gave us strength and helped us accomplish so many of our objectives—and have fun while doing so.

5

Setting Goals

*I have brought myself by long meditation to the conviction
that a human being with a settled goal must accomplish it,
and that nothing can resist a will which will stake
even existence upon its fulfillment.*
—Benjamin Disraeli

Goals create a sense of focus and direction. A team without goals often is interested only in getting the season over with. There is no excitement or anticipation. The prevailing atmosphere is one of hopelessness and resignation. A team with a strong desire to achieve specific goals generates a sense of purpose, mission, and energy.

Until the early 1990s, our team goals were generally set by the coaching staff. We assumed that the coaches knew better than the players what our team was capable of accomplishing and what our priorities should be. After three consecutive disappointing seasons in 1989, 1990, and 1991, I decided that major adjustments were necessary. It wasn't so much that our record was bad in those seasons; we finished 10–2 in 1989, and won nine games in each of the 1990 and 1991 seasons. The disturbing thing was that we tailed off at the end of each season and did not display the drive and focus in bowl games that we needed.

As a staff, we decided that part of the problem might be related to our goal-setting procedures. We recognized that having the coaching staff set team goals gave the players the impression they were being asked to accomplish objectives that were important to the coaching staff but had little to do with what the athletes wanted to achieve. As a result, there was less accountability on the part of the players.

In 1992, in an effort to have the players take ownership of their objectives, we let the players set team goals. As the season began, we asked each player to list in order of importance five goals he felt were critical to the success of the team. We then compiled the goals listed and ranked them according to the frequency each goal was mentioned. Since 1992, with minor variations, the goals listed each year by the players have remained somewhat constant. In 1997, the last Nebraska team I coached listed the following objectives:

Nebraska Football 1997 Team Goals
1 National champions—win Orange Bowl
2 No off-field incidents
3 Big 12 champions
4 Unity
5 Play one game at a time
6 Be the most physically and mentally prepared team in the country
7 Team grade point average—2.85 or higher
8 Undefeated season

Winning the national championship was the goal mentioned most frequently by the players. The only way Nebraska could win the national championship was to go to the Orange Bowl and win it, as the Orange Bowl was the top game in the Bowl Alliance in 1997. The Bowl Alliance was an agreement among all Division IA football teams that required the two top-ranked teams at season's end to play for the national championship. The only difficulty with the plan was that the Big 10 and Pac 10 decided not to join the Alliance. We could only hope that one or both of the two top-rated teams were not in those leagues.

It is significant that winning the national championship was the goal given the highest priority by the players. It was mentioned on nearly every player's list and was, in most cases, at the top of the list. This indicated a high level of confidence and a willingness to make whatever sacrifices were necessary to be the top team in the nation.

Second, the players wanted no off-the-field incidents to reflect poorly on the football team. Most of the team recalled the media criticism we endured throughout the 1995 season and were extremely sensitive to how even one or two incidents could reflect negatively on our entire team. Our players did not want to endure that criticism again. Since the second most frequently mentioned goal concerned off-field behavior, it was obvious that this was a major concern. Actions that embarrassed the team would be subject to peer sanctions from within the team.

Winning the Big 12 championship was the third goal of the 1997 season. We had failed to win the Big 12 championship in 1996, the first year of the Big 12 Conference's existence—we lost to Texas in the championship game in St. Louis. As the 1997 season began, the loss to Texas still stung. The players knew it would be impossible to win the national championship if we did not win the conference title.

The fourth goal was unity. From his first day as a freshman, each player was continually reminded of how important team unity was in accomplishing our overall goals. The players understood that playing together as a unit and getting along well both on and off the field was a high priority. Positive, constructive comments among the players and coaches alike were instrumental in developing and maintaining unity.

In addition to working together, this team was determined to play their best one game at a time. Recognizing the influence college football polls have on deciding the national champion, we knew that each game was critical. We only had to think back to the loss in the Big 12 championship game the year before to realize just how important each game was. Essentially, the season becomes a playoff, as even one loss will make it very hard to win a national championship. Two losses eliminate a team from having any chance at a national championship. There is little margin for error at the top level.

A national championship team must have the maturity and focus to prepare and play well every week, something that is very hard to do. Subjected to emotional highs and lows, human beings are not wired in a way that makes consistent performance easy. The whole season can be ruined by one Saturday of lackluster football brought on by a mental or emotional letdown by the team.

There are many advocates of a playoff to determine the national champion in college football. In professional football, basketball, and baseball—all sports with a playoff—a team can lose several games and still make the playoff with a chance to win a championship. This greater tolerance for failure in the regular season often leads to less intensity until the playoffs. A college football team trying to win it all must give a solid effort every week or the wheels come off very quickly.

The players were also committed to exceptional physical and mental preparation. This goal reflected the players' awareness of the importance of having a great work ethic. The athletes knew that paying a price in the weight room, at practice, and in meetings would be key elements in winning a national championship. Vince Lombardi once said, "The will to prepare to win is even more important than the will to win." There is no question that great teams prepare well Monday through Friday. Teams that do not practice with intensity on a daily basis struggle to maintain the level of consistency necessary to be a championship team.

Academic achievement was also significant to the players. They set a goal of having a team grade point average of 2.85 or better on a four-point scale. I was pleased to see the players make team grade point average a priority. As a staff, we spent a great deal of time emphasizing the importance of academic issues. This goal indicated that they understood they were attending college to get an education and had a tradition to uphold. They were proud of the fact that the graduation rate among Nebraska football players was consistently the best in our conference. The players also appreciated the fact that we had more academic All-Americans in football than any other school in the nation. Many players who entered our program, aware of Nebraska's history of producing academic All-Americans, worked hard to put themselves in position to be so honored as juniors or seniors.

Finally, the players wanted to have an undefeated season. Although this goal appears to be inherent in the pursuit of a national title, there have been occasions where the national championship team had one loss. In order to lose a game and still win a national championship, however, that one loss must occur early in the season, as a late-season loss invariably drops a team too far in the polls to regain the top spot. In Division I, there are usually no more than one or two undefeated teams at the end of the season, so realizing this final goal would put us in fast company.

The 1997 team goals were very high. In fact, I found them to be a little frightening. It is important that goals be challenging, yet attainable. If we lost a game or two early in the season, most of the goals would be impossible to reach. This often results in players feeling they have nothing left to play for. If objectives are lacking, the probability of a serious downward spiral looms large. Each year there are teams that have lofty expectations but, after an early loss, lose their focus and finish with losing seasons.

The positive side of these high standards was that the players accepted accountability by articulating the goals. They believed in their ability to achieve the goals and were willing to pay a great price to accomplish them.

The 1997 team accomplished every goal it set, except for having no off-the-field incidents. One player was involved in an altercation after our regular season had ended. He was suspended from the team for the bowl game, as the players had been warned repeatedly that such conduct would not be tolerated. We finished the season one incident short of meeting every goal that the players had set, a remarkable accomplishment.

Team goals are broad. They provide a sense of direction and mission. However, in order to meet team goals, it is important that more specific, short-term goals be set. They become the building blocks of final objectives.

I attribute a large part of Nebraska's success, particularly in the 1990s, to specific offensive, defensive, and kicking goals that the coaches and players took very seriously. Contrary to team goals, the specific goals for offense, defense, and kicking were set by the coaches. We did not pick numbers out of the air. We studied national statistics concerning every aspect of football. Based on those numbers, we set goals that would rank Nebraska at or near the top nationally in each category. The following were our 1997 offensive goals:

Nebraska Football Offensive Goals
1 Six or more yards average per rushing attempt
2 Pass completions: 55 percent or more
3 Average per pass attempt: 7.0 yards or more
4 Scoring: 40 points or more per game
5 Interception ratio: 4 percent or less

6 Three big plays of 25 yards or more per game
7 One or no turnovers per game
8 Sacks: 5 percent or less of pass attempts
9 Third- and fourth-down conversion: 45 percent or more
10 Score in red zone: 90 percent or more of the time
11 Penalties: 20 yards or less per game
12 Knockdowns: 1.5 or more per play

We believed that a highly productive running game was of primary importance. The number-one offensive goal was to average six yards or more per rushing attempt. Achieving this goal meant that all phases of the offensive team needed to perform at a high level. Our offensive line had to be strong enough and quick enough to move the opponent's defensive linemen off the ball, creating running lanes for the backs. Our receivers were expected to block downfield on every play. When receivers look to see if the ballcarrier is going to break loose and then decide to block once the ballcarrier is past the line of scrimmage, it is too late to make an effective block. The only way for a receiver to make a timely block is to give a full-speed effort to knock a defensive back off his feet on every play. The ballcarrier breaks loose only a few times each game; however, when he did break, our receivers were where they needed to be to help. Running backs have to run hard, breaking tackles and gaining yards after contact. The quarterback has to audible plays that give us the best chance of creating a big gain against the defense.

The emphasis on the running game paid off for us. We led the nation in rushing 11 times between 1980 and 1997, and ranked second five other times. In 18 seasons, we never finished lower than fourth.

Wind blows passes off course and makes it very difficult to throw the ball accurately. We play in a part of the country where wind is a major factor perhaps three or four games a year. Therefore, a strong running game was imperative if we were to have a chance to win all of our games, as a heavy reliance on the passing game would make a loss highly probable on those windy days. We believed that a rushing yard was more valuable than a passing yard when it came to winning football games. If one team threw the ball for 300 yards and had no rushing yards and its opponent rushed for 300 yards and had no passing yards (assuming that all other factors in the game were equal), the rushing team would win a vast majority of the time. The running game enables a team to control the ball, convert short-yardage and goal-line situations, and wear down the opposition. Although an effective passing game is important, we believed that our running game needed to be dominant if we were to do well in the Nebraska climate.

The second offensive goal was to complete 55 percent or more of our passes. Our concern was not how many times we threw the ball, but rather how efficient we were when we threw. I recall losing a key game to Oklahoma, 10–9, in Norman in 1965. Oklahoma threw the ball only four times, yet they completed all four passes. Each pass completion occurred at a critical moment and contributed significantly to the Oklahoma win. Although they did not have many passing yards or pass attempts, they still had a great passing game that day. Nebraska often threw the ball no more than 15 times in a game, yet if we completed ten of those passes for three touchdowns, we had a great day throwing the football.

Even though we emphasized the run, we were still very committed to having an efficient passing game. Our quarterbacks and receivers knew that we would usually not throw the ball more than 12 to 20 times a game; therefore, they would need to maximize every throwing opportunity. Each practice, we spent a great deal of time emphasizing concentration and precision in the passing game. Completing 55 percent or more of the passes thrown was one measure of efficiency.

Another goal assessing the efficiency of the passing game was to average seven yards or more on each pass play called in the huddle. We included all pass plays called in the huddle in this statistic, including quarterback sacks, incomplete passes, interceptions, and pass completions. It was important to gain significant yardage when we passed.

We generally had a very efficient passing game because teams were more concerned with our running game. Opponents' defensive backs were very conscious of stopping the run, which created many excellent opportunities for us to throw the football. I can remember Alabama's Bear Bryant saying that one of his reasons for running the wishbone offense was to have such a strong ground game that his receivers were often given single coverage, opponents having committed all but two defensive backs to stopping the run.

In each game, our offensive objective was to score at least 40 points. This goal, however, involved more than the offensive unit. The field position and turnovers generated by the defense, as well as the field position that resulted from the kicking game, were also very important factors in scoring. As a coaching staff, however, we wanted our offensive players to understand that they were expected to score a high percentage of the times they had the football.

Fumbles and interceptions are devastating to an offense. Our goal was to have an interception ratio of 4 percent or less. In order to achieve this goal, we could have no more than one interception for every 25 pass attempts. A team can pass for 500 yards, yet if they throw five or six interceptions, they would be better off if they had not thrown the ball at all. Most of our better offensive teams had interception ratios of less than 2 percent. Great teams are not careless with the football.

Big plays are critical to offensive production. Our goal was to have three or more big plays per game. A "big play" was defined as one that gained 25 yards or more. Gaining 25 yards or more on at least one play of a drive will usually lead to a score. In order to make big plays, we found it was particularly important for everyone, including our backs and linemen, to block downfield. If we did an effective job of blocking downfield, a play that might otherwise have gained only five or ten yards often became a big gain.

Turnovers are the most important statistical category in any football game. A team with vastly superior talent will lose to an inferior opponent if they have too many turnovers. Therefore, our seventh offensive goal was to have one turnover or less per game. In practice, we placed great emphasis on our ballcarriers carrying the ball securely and our quarterbacks not throwing careless passes. We required all ballcarriers to carry the ball high and tight to their bodies so the ball could not be pulled or punched out of their grasps. It is very important to avoid stating goals negatively, such as "don't fumble" or "don't throw an interception"; such expressions put negative images in the players' minds. Instead, we simply reminded our players of how to properly carry and throw the football, correcting bad habits in practice and encouraging our players in pregame preparations.

If we turned the ball over no more than one time in a ballgame, we believed that we would have a good chance of defeating every opponent we played. Anytime we turned the ball over three times or more, we were in great danger of losing.

Sacks kill drives. We wanted to limit quarterback sacks to 5 percent or less of our pass plays. A sack often ends an offensive possession, as the offense loses a productive down and also suffers a substantial loss. In 1995, we played the entire season without allowing a single sack, an almost unheard-of accomplishment. Tommie Frazier, our quarterback, consistently displayed excellent mobility, strength, and judgment behind a talented offensive line.

Third- and fourth-down conversions are critical. Converting a high percentage of third and fourth downs into first downs allows a team to maintain possession of the ball and keeps drives alive. Our goal was to achieve a 45 percent or better conversion rate; this statistic would normally lead our conference and would rank very high nationally.

In order to score touchdowns and make first downs in short-yardage situations, we worked hard on goal-line and short-yardage plays throughout the week. We even had a live goal-line scrimmage of six or eight plays between our top offensive and defensive players each Wednesday. The goal-line scrimmage was the only full-contact drill of the practice week.

We also paid special attention to third-down, long-yardage situations. We analyzed our opponent's tendencies on all long-yardage downs and emphasized five or six pass plays and three or four running plays that would be particularly effective against the anticipated long-yardage defensive alignments.

The tenth goal was to score in the red zone (the area from the 20-yard line to the goal line) 90 percent or more of the time. It was imperative that once we got close to the opponent's goal that we scored in some fashion, whether it be a touchdown or a field goal. We often changed our offensive play selection in the red zone, as defensive teams tend to blitz linebackers and play more man-to-man pass defense in this area of the field. Option plays and misdirection passes were very effective against blitzing defenses and man-to-man coverage. Our proficiency in this area of the field was usually excellent.

Limiting offensive penalties to 20 yards or less per game was another important goal. This required great discipline and concentration. We practiced twice a week with loudspeakers set at a high volume to acclimate the players to crowd noise (much to the consternation of faculty members teaching late-afternoon classes near the stadium). As a result, we had very few games in which we could not deal with raucous crowds. We used game officials three times a week in our practices. The officials flagged any violations they saw, which kept our players aware of playing within the rules. We were usually the least penalized team in our conference. This was due in large part to the way in which we practiced.

Our final offensive goal was to knock opponents off their feet an average of one and a half times or more per play. This may not sound like an astounding figure; however, good defensive teams are drilled to stay on their feet. We found that if we averaged putting one and a half players on the ground on each offensive play, we would be highly successful. This meant that our offensive line put great emphasis on trying to knock down, or "pancake," opponents. Our backs took great pride in blocking so aggressively that they knocked defenders down. Our receivers blocked downfield on every play in an effort to knock down as many defensive backs as possible. If we ran 70 offensive plays in a game, we expected to knock opponents down at least 105 times to meet our goal. In some games, we had as many as 130 or 140 "knockdowns." On those days, we were very productive offensively.

The players had Sunday off to relax and get away from the pressures of football. On Monday, the first thing we did in our team meeting was review the offensive, defensive, and kicking goals. We projected each goal on a large screen and checked off our failures and successes as we analyzed game results.

On a few occasions, the offensive team achieved all 12 goals. More typically, we accomplished eight or nine offensive goals and still felt we had a solid performance. When we achieved six or fewer goals, we knew we were not playing very well offensively. Even though we might have won by a lopsided margin, our offensive players came to realize that the number of goals we accomplished was a more accurate reflection of our performance than the final score.

Goals have relevance only if the players understand the goals and see how those goals are related to their performance. Our players could see clearly how accomplishing our offensive goals translated into moving the football and winning games. Therefore, they were often either pleased or dejected on Mondays, depending on how many goals they achieved. Most important, the goals affected how we practiced. As players practiced with an awareness of accomplishing specific goals, they developed habits that served them well throughout the season.

Our defense also had a number of specific, performance-related goals. Defensive goals are often the opposite of offensive goals, as the objectives of an offensive unit are precisely those things that a defense does not want to allow.

Our 1997 defensive goals were as follows:

Nebraska Football Defensive Goals

1 Three yards or less average per rushing attempt
2 Passing-defense efficiency: 100.0 or fewer ratings points
3 Total yards given up: 285.0 or less
4 Hold opponent under 13 points per game
5 Give up one or no big plays of 25 yards or more
6 Sack the opposing quarterback an average of one out of eight attempts
7 Intercept an average of one of 17 pass attempts
8 Gain three or more turnovers per game
9 Stop 70 percent of third-down plays
10 Prevent touchdowns 70 percent of time inside red zone
11 Gain possession three times or more per game inside the 50-yard line

As with our offensive emphasis on running the ball, we believed that a great defensive effort starts with stopping the run. Our primary defensive goal was to hold our opponents to three yards or less average per rushing attempt. If our opponent was able to maintain ball control by running the ball up and down the field, our defense would wear down and our offense would seldom have the ball. Therefore, stopping the run defensively was as important to our defense as a great running game was to our offense.

The second defensive goal reflected the efficiency of our pass defense. This statistic is computed based on a complex interaction of several pass-defense factors, such as interceptions, completions, and yards per passing attempt. If the total score in this category was under 100 points, we were playing very good pass defense. Many fans believe that pass defense depends only on the four defensive backs. Actually, pass defense also depends on a great pass rush by the defensive line and good intermediate coverage combined with timely blitzes by the linebackers. All 11 defensive players play a major role in pass defense.

If we were able to hold our opponent to 285 yards or less of total offense per game, we knew we were playing outstanding defense. We found that holding our opponents under 285 yards would consistently rank us among the very top defenses in the nation.

A successful defense not only limits an opponent's total yardage, it also prevents the opposition from scoring. Our goal was to hold our opponents to fewer than 13 points a game. Again, such a statistic would put us at or near the top of national statistics. Generally speaking, if our opponents scored fewer than 13 points, we would win, as there were very few games in which we did not score more than 13 points. Not giving up big plays and playing great goal-line defense were two major keys to preventing opponents from scoring.

The fifth goal was to give up no more than one big play of 25 yards or more. A highly disciplined defense makes few errors and gives up few big plays. Usually, big plays result from a defensive error. Getting our players lined up correctly and clearly communicating the defensive alignment was critical in minimizing defensive errors and giving up big plays.

One of our most ambitious defensive goals was to sack the opposing quarterback one out of every eight pass attempts. Any team throwing the ball 32 times gave up four quarterback sacks when we achieved our goal. Tackling the opposing quarterback in the backfield on a passing play generally results in stopping the opponent's drive. The threat of a sack tends to unnerve the quarterback, causing him to rush his throws.

The seventh defensive goal was to intercept one out of every 17 passes thrown against us. If a team threw 34 times in a game, we expected to intercept the ball at least twice. Most interceptions occur when the quarterback is under pressure and forced to release the ball before his feet are set and he has a good view of the field. Hence, a strong pass rush contributes to interceptions.

As stated previously, the biggest statistic in any game is turnovers. Our defense focused on stripping the ball from ballcarriers, dislodging the ball from receivers, and breaking quickly to intercept passes. Effectively practicing these techniques helped us attain our goal of getting three or more turnovers from our opponent in each game. Statistically, very few teams who get that number of turnovers from their opponents lose a game. The only time a team might lose after gaining three turnovers, everything else being even, would be if that team's own offense turned the ball over three or more times as well.

Our ninth defensive goal was to stop 70 percent of third-down plays short of the first-down marker. Third-down conversions are critical to an offensive team, and third-down stops are equally important to a defensive team. The more a defensive team can limit the opposing offense to "three downs and out," the more opportunity that team's offense has to move the ball.

Preventing a touchdown 70 percent of the time inside the red zone was our tenth defensive goal. The "red zone," defensively, is the area of the field from the 20-yard line to the goal line. Once a team penetrated our 20-yard line, we wanted to play with even greater intensity and concentration. Our secondary had less territory to defend in that area of the field, so we could be more reckless in playing tight coverage on receivers and using more blitzes.

Our final goal was to gain possession of the football three or more times per game inside the 50-yard line. Achieving this objective gave our offense excellent field position, thereby enhancing our chances of scoring. Most fans do not fully realize that field position is a major factor in putting points on the scoreboard. If an offensive team starts on its own ten-yard line and has to go 90 yards to the end zone, the odds of scoring a touchdown are slim.

Starting a drive with less than 50 yards to the goal line significantly increases a team's chances of scoring.

The 11 defensive goals broke down each aspect of defense into components our players could understand. Practicing with those goals in mind made us a strong defensive team. We believed that the more specific we were with our players in setting goals, and the more they bought into the importance of achieving each goal, the better our chances of having a great team were.

Kicking is the third, and often the most ignored, phase of a football game. It is just as important as a team's offense or defense. Even though it is rarely given as much attention by fans, the press, and even some coaches, the kicking game dictates field position, and field position usually dictates who wins the game. The 1997 kicking goals were as follows:

Nebraska Football Kicking Goals

1. Net punting average: 40 yards or more per game (offense)
2. Average punt return: ten yards or more per game (defense)
3. Kickoff coverage: average holding the opponent inside the 23-yard line
4. Kickoff return: average 28-yard line or more
5. Successfully kick 75 percent of all field goal attempts
6. Successfully kick all extra-point attempts
7. No blocked kicks on offense
8. Six or more blocked kicks per season on defense

When we punted the ball, our objective was to net 40 yards or more. The net punt is the distance the ball is punted minus the punt-return yardage. Therefore, net punting included a combination of how far we kicked the ball and how well we covered the kick. One season, our opponents ended up with minus yards on punt returns. Our punt coverage was so good that our opponents had no significant punt returns and actually lost yards several times. This was one of the most memorable kicking-game feats that I recall.

We put our best athletes on our punt-coverage team. Often the coverage team was composed mostly of linebackers, defensive backs, and offensive backs. These people had speed, mobility, and tackling ability. It was imperative that the punter consistently kick the ball high enough that we had time to get down under the punt and make the tackle. A low, line-drive punt is a liability to any coverage team. The ball gets down the field so quickly that the punt coverage can't get there at the same time that the ball arrives.

Second, we attempted to average ten yards or more per punt return. The net effect of a punt is the critical factor. A ten-yard average return on every punt would give us a significant advantage in field position. Johnny Rodgers, the 1972 Heisman Trophy winner, was the best punt returner I have ever seen. John had great lateral movement and an ability to make people miss tackles in the open field. His returns made the difference in several key games en route to Nebraska national championships in 1970 and 1971.

The third kicking goal was to keep our opponent inside the 23-yard line every time we kicked off. Accomplishing this goal depended not only on the ability of the kickoff man to kick the ball deep and high, but also on the speed and aggressiveness of the athletes covering the kicks. We told our players that the most important play of a football game was the opening kickoff, emphasizing that it often set the tone for the game. I'll never forget the opening kickoff return in our game against the University of Oklahoma in 1968. Oklahoma kicked off and covered with such speed and ferocity that they ran over our blockers and annihilated our return man deep in our own territory. Several players were shaken up on the play and our return man lost some teeth. Our team realized that we had an opponent on our hands who would not be denied. Oklahoma ended up beating us 47–0—the worst defeat Nebraska ever suffered under Bob Devaney.

Our fourth kicking goal was to average returning kickoffs to the 28-yard line or beyond. The five-yard difference between the opponent returning kickoffs to the 23-yard line or less and our returning kickoffs to at least the 28-yard line may not seem significant. However, in the course of a game, there were often eight to ten kickoffs. A difference of only five yards per kickoff often resulted in a field-position advantage that resulted in a touchdown.

Many times a field goal is the deciding factor in a close game. Our goal was to make 75 percent of all field goal attempts. Accurate field goal kicking depends on a good snap by the center, a good hold by the holder, good protection, and an accurate field goal kicker. Had we converted on a last-second field goal versus Florida State in the 1994 Orange Bowl game, we would have won a national championship. Kicking often doesn't seem important until a team experiences something like that.

In 1973, my first season as head coach at Nebraska, we played Missouri in the fifth game of the season. Both Nebraska and Missouri were undefeated, but Missouri had been unimpressive in its wins. I recall one of our assistant coaches declaring the night before the game that Missouri was the worst 4–0 team he had ever seen. The next day, after two long Missouri kickoff returns, a fumbled Nebraska punt at our own five-yard line, and a blocked Nebraska field goal, Missouri was 5–0 and we were 4–1. We had outplayed Missouri decisively on offense and defense, outyarding them two to one. Yet Missouri won the game 13–12, almost solely on their superior kicking game.

The sixth goal was to successfully kick all extra-point attempts. A blocked or missed extra point is often the deciding factor at the end of a football game.

Since a blocked kick could change the momentum of a game more quickly than any other play, our seventh goal was to have no blocked kicks on offense. We averaged having a kick blocked only once every three or four years. There was no excuse to ever have a blocked kick. We worked hard on our punt protection and field goal protection and spent a great deal of time of making sure that our kickers kicked the ball quickly. Developing a center who can get the snap back to the kicker with speed and accuracy is a major factor in avoiding blocked kicks.

The final kicking goal for Nebraska was to block six or more kicks per season. These blocked kicks could be punts, field goals, or extra-point tries. It takes a special ability for a player to keep his eyes open and put his hands on the ball as it is kicked. Most players will shut their eyes and turn their heads at a critical moment.

Baron Miles, a walk-on cornerback who played for us in the early 1990s, was the best player I have ever seen at blocking kicks. He had a unique ability to focus on the ball as it left the kicker's foot. I can still see Baron literally taking the ball off the punter's foot in a key play at Oklahoma State in 1993 that resulted in a Nebraska touchdown. We were struggling at that point in the game, and the blocked kick was a major factor in our winning the game.

We were fortunate in being able to meet our goal of six blocked kicks a season on several occasions. Going through a season without one of our kicks being blocked, as well as blocking six or more of our opponents' kicks, often enabled us to win games we would not have won otherwise.

We continually emphasized the importance of the kicking game to the players, particularly in a game where two teams were evenly matched. In most seasons, the kicking game would make the difference in at least two or three football games. If we had a poor kicking game and everything else was even, we would lose. On the other hand, if we had an outstanding kicking game and our opponent did not, we would generally win. Fortunately, we usually had the best kicking game.

The players understood that we put our best athletes on the kicking teams. Often those on kicking teams are perceived as second-rate players who are used to save wear and tear on front-line players. We often had All-American players on our kicking teams, because we believed that kicking plays are pivotal in each football game. Being on a kicking team was seen as a privilege and not as a demotion.

We also practiced our kicking game in the middle of practice, rather than at the end of practice, as many teams do. Putting kicking at the end of practice, often when players are fatigued and not focusing, implies that kicking is not very important. The emphasis we placed on the kicking game resulted in the players taking this aspect of the game very seriously.

One of the interesting things about football is that a team gets feedback every week as to how they are performing. In many business endeavors, it is difficult to assess performance, as feedback is often sporadic and unclear. Some projects are in progress for months, even years, before results begin to take shape. There

were times when I, as a coach, wished we didn't have to be evaluated so frequently or so publicly. This constant scrutiny was
often wearing; but, on the other hand, life was never dull. The
number of goals accomplished each week provided us with feedback as to how well we were playing much more accurately than
did media accounts or fan reaction.

In examining our weekly goals, one can sense Nebraska's
football philosophy. Vince Lombardi once described football as a
"spartan game," and that is how we played. We placed a premium
on blocking and tackling. We required a very physical, disciplined
approach to the game and expected our players to pay a greater
physical price than the teams we played. Rather than relying on
finesse, we adopted a blue-collar mentality. The players adapted
well to this style of football and were determined to be more
aggressive and better conditioned than our opponents.

By reviewing our performance each Monday, the players
observed the interaction of offensive, defensive, and kicking
goals. Each goal was significant to the overall effectiveness of the
football team. A great offense without the field position that the
defense could provide was never as effective as it might have
been. A defense that was on the field most of the time because
of the offense's inability to sustain drives would soon wear down
no matter how strong it was. The kicking game was critical to
field position. Both the offensive and the defensive teams did
much better if our opponents spent most of the game in their
own territory.

Early in our Monday meeting, the entire team looked at
the tape of the kicking plays. Emphasizing the kicking game
at the beginning of the first meeting of the week demonstrated
to the players that it was the glue that held everything together.
Kicking-game results represented team attitude more than any
other phase of the game did.

This discussion of goals relates to most organizations involved
in competitive endeavors. The objectives and approaches presented
may serve as a model for incorporating both long-term and short-
term goals.

Experience taught our organization the importance of empow-
ering the individuals who must accomplish goals by involving
them in the goal-setting process. Having clearly stated this, specific

goals contribute to effective performance. A regular review of goals and assessing progress in relation to those goals are also very important. Without consistent feedback, it is easy to stray from the organization's primary objectives.

It is important to have short-term goals broken down into components that enable one to see a clear relationship between daily activities and organizational objectives. As we reviewed our offensive, defensive, and kicking goals each Monday, our players could see what they specifically needed to work on during the week of practice. The more players took ownership of short-term and long-term goals, the more effective our team became.

Lou Holtz, former Notre Dame football coach, recognized the importance of goal setting. "All winning teams are goal-oriented. . . . Teams like these win consistently because everyone connected with them concentrates on specific objectives. They go about their business with blinders on; nothing will distract them from achieving their aims."

Our players and coaches developed a strong faith in the goal-setting process. They came to realize that as each segment of the team accomplished specific goals weekly, the better we became and the more likely we were to win.

6

Paying a Price

They may outsmart me, or be luckier,
but they can't outwork me.
—Woody Hayes, former college football coach

The importance of a strong work ethic was something I learned at an early age. I recall my father talking about the time he contracted to shovel coal from a railroad car on an extremely hot day during the Depression. He explained how he had stopped perspiring at one point and knew that he was not doing well physically. However, he finished the job and suffered an episode of acute heat exhaustion. Although what he did was not wise, he often made the point that you should finish any project you start and that it is important to work hard for anything you want to accomplish.

Even though I did not grow up in a poverty-stricken family, we did not have a great deal of material wealth. I was encouraged to go to work when I was 11 years old. I started my own lawn mowing service in the summers and can remember using a hand mower to mow several lawns for 50 cents an hour. I'm sure the yards were no more than average size, but they seemed huge and the time required to mow one of them interminable. When I became old enough, I worked on construction crews in the summers and came to the conclusion that it was a good idea to get an education so I would not spend the rest of my life in construction work.

This work ethic transferred to the athletic field, as well. As a sophomore in high school, I loved running the hurdles in track. However, I suffered a muscle sheath injury that prevented me from lifting my lead leg over the hurdles effectively and the track coaches moved me to the 440-yard dash (now the 400-meter dash). I played basketball, which involved conditioning, but not the same kind of conditioning that track required; therefore, I was never in good track condition when the season started, and it was usually late in the track season before I became at all acclimated to running the race. The 440 was a very difficult race for me in that I was relatively tall and the last 150 yards of the race were always excruciating. I usually felt like quitting at about the 300-yard mark, but never did.

I hated the 440, yet I continued to run it through high school and all four years of college. Looking back on it, I don't believe that it was wise to force myself to do something that was so distasteful. It would have been good to have at least one season where I was removed from athletic competition so I could recuperate. The work ethic and the need to finish what I started stayed with me, almost to an unhealthy degree.

Forcing myself to do the hard things, even things I did not enjoy, was seen as a virtue. I believed that paying a great price in and of itself had merit. This somewhat compulsive work ethic got things done, but not without a spiritual price. As a young man, I was not impacted by the concept of grace—the idea that we are accepted and loved by God just as we are and that God's approval does not need to be earned, it is simply there. God's grace has become more real as I have grown older. This concept has helped me to be more forgiving of myself and those around me, but vestiges of the old driven nature still persist to an uncomfortable degree. Finding a balance between a desire to accomplish something with one's life and an understanding of the gift of grace, which can never be earned, is not easy.

People who observed our football program often commented to me that the most impressive feature of the program was the work ethic of the players. Pro scouts who saw many other teams practice, new coaches who joined our staff having coached elsewhere, and TV analysts who watched our practices all said that players at Nebraska paid a greater price than players at almost any other school they observed.

These people were impressed by the dedication and the work ethic exhibited by our team. This was not just true during the football season. It started during the latter part of January each year, as we began our off-season conditioning program. Owing to weather conditions in Nebraska, we conducted these workouts in our indoor practice area. We had a six-week period where weight lifting, agility drills, and stretching exercises were emphasized in an effort to develop stronger, quicker athletes.

I believe that the success or failure of a team is at least 75 percent determined even before practice begins in the fall. Most people think the season starts in early August. However, the team that has prepared exceptionally well in the off-season and improved the most in speed, strength, and agility already has a distinct advantage when the season begins.

Since the late 1960s, Boyd Epley, Nebraska's strength and conditioning coach, has been the chief architect of the off-season program. Boyd was originally a pole vaulter on the track team but became more and more interested in weight lifting. He developed size and strength and started to break so many pole vaulting poles that the track coach encouraged him to find another sport. Boyd found that his true interest was more in the strength and conditioning area than in track and field. Bob Devaney had the foresight to hire Boyd at a time when few schools were interested in weight training. I don't believe that any school had a full-time strength and conditioning coach at that time. Bob's decision to hire Boyd was influenced by Nebraska's losing two key bowl games rather badly to Alabama. In both games, Alabama's quickness proved to be the decisive factor.

The Orange Bowl Committee used to require both participating teams to stay one extra day to attend a party held the night after the bowl game. I vividly recall Bear Bryant introducing his team at the 1966 Orange Bowl party. He seemed to enjoy stating the height and weight of each player, particularly his linemen, most of whom weighed less than 200 pounds and weren't very tall. Those Orange Bowl parties were extravagant and nice for the winners but were really agonizing for the losing team. I watched Bob Devaney wince as Coach Bryant bragged about his "little" players.

Alabama had an extensive off-season program designed to develop quickness and agility. Strength, however, was not an integral part of their conditioning program at that time. Boyd designed a conditioning program for us that incorporated all three aspects: agility, quickness, and strength.

This training regimen certainly began to pay dividends. We had great football teams in 1970 and 1971 and won national championships both years. Ironically, our record went to 13–0 as we beat Alabama 38–6 in January 1972 to clinch the national championship. In the process, Bob Devaney may have taught Bear Bryant a lesson: Quickness and agility are important, but if you have players who are big, strong, *and* quick and agile, they will perform very well against a quick, small team.

Bob loved a good party after a win. I can still remember Bob dancing and celebrating at the party after the 1972 Orange Bowl. Bob had won the national championship the year before as we defeated LSU 17–12 in the Orange Bowl. That win over LSU was great, but I could tell that the win over Alabama and Bear Bryant was the highlight of Bob's coaching career.

Curiously, Bear Bryant was voted Coach of the Year by the American Football Coaches Association that year. At that time, the vote was held prior to the bowl games. Not long after that, the vote was moved to a date after the bowls were played. If this had been the case in 1972, I'm sure that Bob would have received the honor. Coach of the Year was about the only honor Bob didn't receive in the coaching profession. He certainly deserved it.

Boyd Epley was ahead of his time and remained on the leading edge of expertise in strength and conditioning. Boyd was always a record keeper. He did an outstanding job of maintaining records for all types of activities, such as the 10-yard dash, the 40-yard dash, the agility run, the vertical jump, and all weight-lifting activities. Setting a record in one of these tests became a major source of motivation for our players. From the time they first enrolled at the university through their final year of eligibility, our players were tested on each of those measures three to four times a year. As a result, they could track their progress, and most of them took a good deal of pride in their accomplishments in the conditioning program. These records also allowed coaches to quickly assess whether or not a player was improving.

The off-season workouts became especially focused in the summer. Early in my coaching career, summer workouts were rather sporadic, and only a few players maintained a consistent conditioning program. More recently, players encouraged each other to stay in Lincoln for summer conditioning drills. Each player knew that the other players at his position were working out and realized that if he didn't join them, he would quickly fall by the wayside. Internal competition combined with a strong work ethic were key factors in providing the conditioning edge that Nebraska enjoyed. A player quickly got the picture that if he was not willing to pay a great price, even in the off-season, he would be overtaken by someone who would pay that price. Former St. Louis Hawks forward Ed Macauley observed: "If you are not practicing, just remember—someone, somewhere is practicing and when you two meet, given roughly equal ability, he will win."

If our players worked unusually hard, it may have been partially due to seeing the coaches do the same. We started formal preparation for each upcoming season on August 1 with a series of staff meetings. Within a few days the freshmen reported, and three days later the varsity players arrived. From that point on, the coaching staff did not have a day off until recruiting was over in the middle of February.

We began our staff meetings at 7 A.M. Monday through Friday, and we were often engaged in preparation on Saturday and Sunday mornings, as well. We met as a staff on Sunday and Monday nights and worked individually the remaining nights of the week. During the August through February period, we averaged 85- to 90-hour workweeks.

I did not require anyone to work on Saturday night or Sunday morning. I wanted the coaches to have the option of going to church with their families on Sunday morning. However, the coaches were required to have Saturday's game thoroughly evaluated and graded by early Sunday afternoon, which meant they had to work either Saturday night or Sunday morning. I did a television show on Saturday evenings and often had trouble sleeping the night after a game, so I graded the game tapes late Saturday night. This regimen was demanding, yet no one complained and each coach did his part as the season wore on. The most difficult thing was never having a day off for such a long time.

Once the recruiting season ended in February, we evaluated films of the past season and began considering offensive and defensive changes for the next season. Spring football practice started in late March and lasted most of April. Spring recruiting took place in May. Football camps for high school players took up most of June. July was spent studying films of upcoming opponents and taking some vacation time.

When I started coaching in the 1960s, the season didn't begin until the middle of September and only ten games were on the schedule. Now the season starts earlier, the number of games has increased, and spring recruiting and summer football camps have been added. In addition, coaches are now held accountable for graduation rates, drug testing, and player behavior—and the pressure to win is greater. So things haven't gotten easier.

Hard work is important, but there must be some balance. I found that there was a point where the performance of the staff would start to deteriorate. The coaches were highly motivated professionals, yet they were not machines. Therefore, I thought it was important to not require them to stay in the office at night Tuesday through Friday.

Some head coaches keep their assistants in their offices until midnight all week long and expect them to be back at work by 6 A.M. Some even sleep in their offices. Under such conditions, coaches eventually become resentful, burned out, or both. I have talked to coaches on other staffs who do not see their children for days on end; you can hear the pain in their voices as they discuss their families.

I also found it important not to prescribe busywork. We each had assigned tasks to perform and were very thorough in game preparation and recruiting, but I didn't keep coaches at their desks just for the sake of being there. Once they were finished, they were expected to leave.

Coaching is not a profession for lazy people, and it is rare to find individuals who exhibit such qualities in coaching. Laziness, however, is not as big a problem as workaholism. The temptation is often to work harder, put in longer hours, watch more films, and call more recruits. This temptation gets stronger as the championship eludes you or you fail to win the "big game" one more time.

My wife, Nancy, and I always tried to reserve some time for each other on Thursday nights, yet I found myself cutting into those nights and sometimes eliminating this time together entirely. There was a constant tension between doing what the job demanded, reserving some time for your family, and getting enough rest to stay mentally sharp. Striking a balance was never easy. Balancing a demanding and time-consuming job with family responsibilities is a common dilemma among many people in our culture. I tried to spend as much time as possible with my children when I got home from work. However, our staff worked until 10 P.M. on Sunday and Monday nights; Friday nights I stayed with the team; and Tuesday, Wednesday, and Thursday nights I brought game tapes home to review. This schedule did not leave much time for my family during the season. I attended all of the children's athletic contests that I could possibly get to and, at the time, felt like I was being a good father. In retrospect, however, I recognize missed opportunities with my children that will never present themselves again.

Fortunately, my relationship with my children turned out well as they grew into adults. My wife, Nancy, bore by far the greatest burden of raising them. The one thing I hope that each of them understands is that I truly love them, was always concerned about them, and that my commitment to them never wavered.

Working hard is important; having a clear vision of why one is working hard is even more important. In 1993, our football team finished with an 11–1 record. The one loss was to Florida State in a game that we lost 16–18 after we missed a field goal as time ran out. Florida State had a great team that year, yet we outplayed them in most phases of the game. This loss was devastating because it resulted in losing the national championship. There were so many "ifs" after that game—if we had made the field goal, if a punt return for an apparent touchdown hadn't been called back, if the Florida State fumble into the end zone had been ruled a fumble rather than a touchdown, and so on. Unfortunately, those "ifs" didn't change the final score. All we could do was learn from this game and move on.

As the players started preparing for the 1994 football season in late January, I sensed a different attitude. Our players had always worked hard; however, this year was different. They made no bones about the fact that they were working to win the 1994 national championship. They felt they had deserved the championship the year before, and in 1994 they were going to make sure that they won it. Each agility drill, weight workout, and spring practice reflected the team's dedication to being the top team in the nation at the end of the year. Normally players would work hard in the off-season, but their focus was to finish the workout so they could get on to more enjoyable things once the workout was over. This year, however, was different. This team was on a mission. They were excited about the future. Brutus Hamilton, Olympic track coach, observed, "It is one of the strange ironies of this strange life . . . those who work the hardest, who subject themselves to the strictest discipline, who give up certain pleasurable things in order to achieve a goal, are the happiest men."

When the 1994 season came around, we were ready. Then we lost Tommie Frazier, our starting quarterback, for almost the whole season with blood clots in his leg. Brook Berringer stepped in for Tommie at quarterback and played exceptionally well for a quarterback with little previous experience. Then Brook went down with a collapsed lung on two successive weeks. The injuries were devastating, yet somehow we kept winning. The work ethic and the resolve were so strong that we finished the season 13–0 and beat Miami in the Orange Bowl for the national championship.

The win over Miami in the Orange Bowl on their home field was especially meaningful. Several ghosts from the past were exorcised in that game. Miami had been almost unbeatable on its home field for more than a decade. They had won more than 60 home games while losing only once. The humidity was always a problem in Miami, particularly for a northern team late in the year. Yet we won the game in the fourth quarter, coming from behind to beat a team that had beaten us in the Orange Bowl three times previously in the 1980s and 1990s.

There is no doubt that the drive and energy generated during the 1994 season came from the common vision that permeated our team. Our work ethic was outstanding. The objective was clear and the players' hard work was focused on one single goal: the national championship. This work ethic and focus made us a team that was very hard to beat. As Vince Lombardi once said, "The harder you work, the harder it is to surrender."

The 1994 season was not the last time I observed the importance of having a clearly identified objective. I mentioned earlier that our players were disappointed with the 1996 season, even though we ended the season with a victory in the Orange Bowl over Virginia Tech and finished with an 11–2 record. Many of our athletes had played in consecutive national championship games following the 1993, 1994, and 1995 seasons. The 1996 season was a letdown in spite of some excellent accomplishments.

Defensive standouts Jason Peter and Grant Wistrom, along with quarterback Scott Frost, provided great leadership for the 1997 season. The 1997 off-season workouts mirrored those of the 1994 season in terms of intensity and commitment. One summer day I was walking from the weight room back to my office. Summer conditioning drills were being conducted, and my path took me past the football field. I was surprised to see Jason Peter run 30 yards to tackle a player participating in another drill. The players were in sweat clothes, and no physical contact ever occurred in such a setting. I called Jason over and asked him what was going on, as someone could have been hurt. Jason told me that he had seen the player loafing and that he felt the player was letting the team down. I told Jason that we couldn't have that sort of thing and asked him to apologize to the player he had tackled.

Even though I didn't approve of what Jason did, I couldn't argue with his level of commitment. Jason and his teammates were on a mission. They wanted to be in the national championship game in Miami on January 2, 1998. Their undefeated season and playing Tennessee in the Orange Bowl for a national championship were not by accident.

How did we end up with such a commitment to excellence among our players and staff? I have no quick and easy answers; however, I believe that the walk-on program was a major contributing factor. A walk-on, almost by definition, is someone possessing a great work ethic. Walk-on players come to Nebraska without a scholarship in hopes of proving that they are capable of playing major college football. A surprisingly large number of them were able to do this. Our travel squad consisted of 60 players, and, on average, 20 of those 60 players came as walk-ons. Normally six to eight players who walked on were among our 22 starters. Most of those walk-ons were from small towns and rural areas in Nebraska and had a good understanding of what hard work is all about. They were willing to make sacrifices to achieve something they felt was important, and in Nebraska, playing football at the University of Nebraska was considered to be very important.

Many people were amazed at the number and the quality of the walk-ons at Nebraska. There were some who maintained that we had "county" scholarships. Several coaches at other schools believed that each county in the state of Nebraska provided a full scholarship for a "walk-on" to play football at Nebraska. Of course, this would be a major NCAA violation and such scholarships didn't exist. However, the rumor persisted, and the fact that we had numerous walk-ons playing gave credence to the rumor.

Nebraska is somewhat unusual among big colleges, being the only Division I football school in the state. We were not involved in an "in-state rivalry," which often leads to marginal players being offered scholarships for fear the rival school will scholarship them first. We did, however, offer scholarships to every football player in the state who came reasonably close to being a quality Division I player. Our theory was that if we were going to make a mistake, it would be with a Nebraska player.

There are many players who have the potential to mature into Division I players after two or three years of hard work. Nearly 50 percent of the in-state players with that ability walked on at Nebraska. Some of them were offered scholarships at Division II and Division III schools and were willing to forgo those scholarships to come to the University of Nebraska without financial aid.

We typically saved three to five scholarships a year for walk-on players. Many schools allocate all of their scholarships to players coming out of high school and do not save scholarships for walk-ons already in their programs. We treated our walk-on players the same as scholarship players in terms of dressing room area, training facilities, equipment, academic services, and, above all, in valuing them as players and people.

In many schools, walk-ons are treated like second-class citizens. A few years ago our coaches visited another school during spring practice. The dressing facilities were a long way from the practice fields. The scholarship players rode to practice on a bus; the walk-on players walked. Most walk-ons don't want the term "walk-on" to be taken so literally. Players pick up on this quickly, and it isn't long before the word gets out that a walk-on is really wasting his time in those programs.

Coaches at some schools who could have a good walk-on program don't want to be bothered with one. The determining factor as to whether or not an athlete decides to walk on is quite often whether he feels he will be given a fair chance and be treated like every other player on the team. The walk-on program was a tremendous asset. With the relatively small population base of the state, walk-ons enabled us to compete with football programs at colleges located in more populated areas.

In general, two-thirds of our squad came from the state of Nebraska. This preponderance of home-state players enabled us to have a team with a strong desire to represent the state well. It is very easy to become so enamored with talented players who come from a distance that home-state talent is ignored. We made sure that Nebraska high school players understood that they were of central importance to our team.

We had a few walk-ons from out of state who came to us through fortuitous circumstances. The first such walk-on I can recall was Langston (Trey) Coleman, who came to Nebraska in the early 1960s. When I first met Trey, I had just arrived at Nebraska as a graduate assistant coach. Trey's mother worked in the Washington, D.C., office of Ted Sorenson, a powerful political figure from Nebraska who recommended that he attend school at Nebraska. Even though Trey was relatively slight, he became a very good defensive end for us because of his competitiveness and great desire.

Two decades later, we were fortunate to have two brothers, Jimmy and Toby Williams, also walk-ons from Washington, D.C. We noticed Jimmy and Toby on a film that had been sent to us by an inner-city Washington, D.C., high school coach. The quality of the film was so poor that we could tell very little about their ability. We wrote them a letter informing them that we couldn't offer them scholarships but would like to have them walk on. The Williams brothers had no other schools showing much interest, so they came to Nebraska and paid their own way. Both of them had great careers and were three-year starters for us. Jimmy was an All-American, and both Jimmy and Toby played a number of years in the NFL. We found that giving encouragement to young men who had potential paid off. Cases like Jimmy and Toby were not all that rare.

One of our most unusual walk-ons was Isaiah Moses Hipp. He went by the initials "I.M." and became a great player for us. In almost every case, walk-on players came to Nebraska because of some encouragement by our coaching staff. However, I.M. showed up on our campus without notice. He was from South Carolina, a state seldom visited by Nebraska recruiters. He had an injury in his senior year of high school and played very little; therefore, he received little attention from college recruiters. He had heard that walk-on players were given a good opportunity at Nebraska and arrived in Lincoln unannounced. His girlfriend financed his trip to Lincoln and gave him enough money to register for classes. He took out a student loan to enable him to get through his first year. By his second year, he had earned a scholarship. During the time he was at Nebraska, he was our best running back and earned all-conference honors; eventually he played a brief time in the National Football League.

Derrie Nelson was a more typical case. Derrie was from Fairmont, Nebraska, a community of only a few hundred people, yet he played great football for us and also had a career in the NFL. There were many others like Derrie. Brothers Jeff and Joel Makovicka were two of our best fullbacks. Both walked on after playing eight-man football at tiny Brainard, Nebraska.

Adam Treu was another walk-on success story. We noticed Adam as a basketball player at Pius X high school in Lincoln. Adam was a rangy 6 feet 6 and 215 pounds at the time. He was definitely not big enough to be a lineman, but he had very good quickness and excellent coordination. We encouraged Adam to walk on, as we were convinced that with maturity and work in the weight room, he could possibly get big enough to play. It was a slow process, but each year Adam put on 15 to 20 pounds and kept getting stronger. By the time he was a senior, he was a great football player. He was our deep snapper and was an outstanding offensive lineman. He also played in the NFL.

The walk-on program provided us with some great first-string players and with some who were solid backup players. The walk-ons added much-needed depth to the team, particularly when NCAA rules cut back scholarships.

Another advantage of the walk-on program was that it gave us enough players to practice differently than most teams. Most college teams have two practice stations. One station has two offensive teams running against a scout team defense; the other station has two defensive teams working against a scout team offense. This practice arrangement results in only half of the offensive and defensive teams practicing at one time. Therefore, many players are standing and watching.

In our practices, we were able to involve many more players than was usually seen in the above-mentioned arrangement. We had our first offense running against scout team defensive players, and, simultaneously, our second offensive team working against another defensive scout team. We also had our first defense working against a scout team offense and our second defense working against a second scout team offense. As a result, we had two offensive units and two defensive units preparing at the same time. This resulted in a great many plays being run during the course of a practice. Our offensive units normally ran 85 to 100 plays during practice—nearly twice as many plays as most Division I teams ran.

A coaching philosophy also governs how teams practice. Many teams have enough players to split their practice up as we have, but are unwilling to do so. There is often a reluctance to divide coaches into more than two groups for practice purposes. Offensive and defensive coordinators often want to have their presence felt at all times during practice. I had enough confidence in all of the members of our staff to divide our coaches among four stations. Even though we had only two offensive coaches at each of the offensive stations and two defensive coaches at each of the defensive stations, those coaches, along with graduate assistants or undergraduate coaches, could do a good job of running the practice. We had the whole practice videotaped and were able to review each play when practice was over. Any team with at least 95 to 100 players, which most Division I football teams have, could split their practice to a greater degree than most of them do.

Having players active the whole time they are on the practice field also had a beneficial conditioning effect. Players worked very hard as they ran the high number of repetitions during practice. No one spent time standing around, which gave us the endurance to be a very good fourth-quarter team. We often had as much activity in an hour-and-a-half practice as occurred in a two-and-a-half-hour practice at other institutions. Such a practice schedule requires a great deal of organization and planning; however, the benefits more than compensate for the added detail work.

The tempo and intensity of our practices was also exceptional. Plays were run rapidly. There was a continual push on the part of the players and coaches to do things correctly and with enthusiasm. On Tuesday and Wednesday practices, we would match the top defense against the top offense. Practicing against scout teams did not result in the same tempo as practicing against first-team players. We practiced our top units this way for only 14 to 15 plays and did not engage in a full-scale scrimmage. However, the blocking in the line was live and pursuit to the ball was full speed. There was always a competitive nature to these drills, and they seemed to help our football team get better as the season went along.

For several years we had kept our top offensive and defensive units separate during practice once we started the season. The scout teams would try to give the top offensive and defensive teams good competition, but would get beaten down physically and were less and less competitive as the season progressed. Practicing in this way did not result in offensive and defensive improvement during the season.

We got the idea of pitting the top units against each other for a short period twice a week from Florida State. We noticed that Florida State seemed to improve more than most teams during the season, so we asked their coaches why this was. Bobby Bowden and his staff helped us out, told us about their practice format, which matched top players against each other for short periods, and we began to play better in the latter stages of the season. We had a good relationship with most schools but exchanged more information with Florida State than any other team.

The type of practice regimen we followed allowed us to play an unusually physical and aggressive style of football. We talked continually to our players about being a physical football team that would pay a greater price than other teams. We expected our receivers to block downfield on every play. Three or four times a game this extra effort resulted in a big play.

Teams who played Nebraska knew that they would be involved in a very physical game. Sometimes this worked to our advantage, as some teams were apprehensive about the game before they stepped on the field.

As I think of the tremendous amount of energy expended year round by our players and coaches, I believe that what we did best was to utilize all of the resources available to us. The walk-ons, the strength and conditioning program, and a great coaching staff all contributed to this effort. We accomplished a great deal while maintaining an enjoyable and reasonably balanced atmosphere.

Drawing a parallel between Division I football and the business world, I would suggest that there may be occasions when resources are not fully utilized. Just as many football teams do not utilize walk-ons, many business organizations may ignore sources of greater productivity. It is very easy to underestimate the talents of employees and assign more administration and supervisors than necessary. As we spread our players and coaches over more practice stations, we increased productivity significantly. Nearly all players were actively engaged in practice and took more responsibility for their performances, since fewer coaches were available to supervise the larger number of practice stations. Given opportunity and encouragement, players with average ability often developed into great players. I would suppose that many businesses might benefit by giving their workforce more responsibility with less supervision, thus increasing productivity and profitability.

Faith in those who work for us and with us is usually conducive to an even stronger work ethic. When people realize that someone has faith in them and is giving them additional responsibility, productivity usually increases. We have a natural desire to not want to disappoint those who believe in us and trust us.

7

Unity

*Develop a state of mind that will concern itself with
everyone on the team. If you do this you will have more than
your share of champions, and fewer of these champions
will have a distorted idea of their own importance.*
—James ("Doc") Counsilman, former swimming coach

The longer I coached, the more convinced I became that the competence of a team could not be judged by adding up the talents of the individual players. It seemed that there was often a synergy that enabled a group of players to exceed their combined talents. Conversely, there were times when teams played at a level less than the sum of all of the individual abilities on the team. But our ideal was to build a whole that could exceed the sum of its parts.

In order to have this synergy, it is important that everyone has a common vision and mission. In a highly competitive endeavor such as football, there are built-in rivalries and animosities that need to be overcome. Sometimes one offensive coach wants to run the ball while another offensive coach wants to emphasize the passing game. Defensive coaches sometimes bicker over the merits of an "attacking" defense versus a "reading" defense. Coaches often have disagreements over recruiting. A coach may have been recruiting a player for some time in his given area of the country only to have another coach look at tapes of the player's high school games and decide that the player is not worthy of a scholarship. This often leads to major disagreements and even some bitterness among members of the staff.

There is often an innate rivalry between offensive and defensive units, which is exacerbated by the competition in spring football. After a spring scrimmage, the press wants to declare a "winner." This need to declare a victor results in stories written about the offense getting the best of the defense or vice versa in a scrimmage. When offensive or defensive pride is wounded, the competition between units tends to heighten. Sometimes this competition can assume an unhealthy proportion and erode team unity.

Some players receive more publicity and attention than others despite the other players' contributing as much to the team's performance. Offensive linemen, for example, often labor in obscurity, yet are as important as players at more highly publicized positions. This disparity of recognition can lead to jealousy and dissension within a football team. If coaches and players adhere to a common philosophy, keep their eyes on important common objectives, and work together, great things can happen. If infighting and turf battles run rampant, the team can easily fall into disarray.

Nebraska had outstanding teams in the early 1980s. In 1981, we won the Big 8 championship and beat Oklahoma soundly in Norman—something that had been very difficult for us to do. In 1982 and 1983, we finished with identical 12–1 records. Each year we beat Oklahoma and won the Big 8 championship. In 1982, our only loss came on a late touchdown drive by Penn State at State College, Pennsylvania. Our one loss in 1983 was a heartbreaker to the University of Miami in the Orange Bowl, as we failed on a two-point conversion at the end of the game. The pass for the two points was slightly deflected and bounced off the shoulder pad of the intended receiver, and we fell in a 31–30 contest. We had been a very dominant football team throughout the season and were ranked number one going into the game. Had we been able to win that final game in the Orange Bowl, we would have clearly been the national champions in 1983.

As the 1980s unfolded, things didn't go as well. In 1989, we had a good team, losing only to the University of Colorado in Boulder during the regular season. We took a 10–1 record into a Fiesta Bowl contest with Florida State, but had several turnovers and were beaten 41–17. The most disappointing aspect of the Fiesta Bowl game was that several of our players violated a team policy of alcohol abstinence while we were in Tempe. Even though the team had voted to stay away from alcohol, several players chose to disregard the policy. Most of the players knew that this violation of policy was occurring, yet nothing was brought to the attention of the coaching staff. This situation created a division within the team, as most of the players felt that those who were using alcohol were not only breaking training but were violating a policy established by the team. We ended the season with a 10–2 record, yet the performance in the Fiesta Bowl left me frustrated and disappointed. It was hard to understand why some players cared so little about the team's welfare that they would deliberately violate team rules at a critical time.

Losing always hurts; however, it is not so painful when there is love, unity, mutual respect, and trust. The bond between players and coaches results in shared sorrow over the loss. The fact that everyone feels as though they are in the loss together somehow seems to ease the pain. The Fiesta Bowl loss was particularly devastating, as it indicated that some of our players had so little pride and respect for the team that they were willing to put partying ahead of team welfare.

After the game, Rich Bell, a senior wingback, told me that some of the players were simply not able to withstand the temptation of the local girls who hung around during our stay in Tempe. Early in our preparations at Arizona, we had been invited to a Fiesta Bowl party at a mock western town called "Rawhide." When we entered the grounds, approximately one hundred young women who had been invited to the event began to attach themselves to various players. They did not disappear for the rest of the stay in Arizona. I realize that the players were at fault for not adhering to team rules, but I made sure from that point on when we went to a bowl game that I knew exactly what parties and entertainment were planned and what the ground rules were. I did not like the setup at "Rawhide" and made sure the next trip to the Fiesta Bowl did not include inviting a large contingent of women who would provide distraction.

In 1990, things didn't improve. After a tough loss to Colorado in Lincoln, we took a 9–1 record into the final game of the season at Oklahoma. Mickey Joseph, our starting quarterback that year, suffered a huge gash in his leg as he was run into a steel bench on the Oklahoma sideline. The injury was serious enough that Mickey required extensive medical attention and was out for the rest of the season. After Mickey's injury, we threw several interceptions and lost decisively to Oklahoma in the season finale, 45–10.

With a 9–2 record, we were relegated to the Citrus Bowl in Orlando to play an excellent Georgia Tech team that was undefeated, confident, and had momentum. Georgia Tech had a good chance of being voted the national champion if they were able to beat Nebraska. I thought our athletes were as talented as Georgia Tech's. However, Tech was playing for a national championship and they had a healthy quarterback. Mickey Joseph had not recovered from the leg injury he had suffered at Oklahoma. We did not play well and lost 45–21, finishing the season with a 9–3 record. Colorado and Georgia Tech tied for the national championship, so two of our three losses were to national championship teams and the third loss was partly attributable to the injury to Mickey Joseph at Oklahoma. However, I was really down after that season. I felt something was missing. The players were not insubordinate and there was not open hostility among the team. However, I sensed a lack of unity and resolve that would be necessary to take us to the top echelon of college football. The cohesion necessary to have a great football team was lacking; the chemistry just wasn't right.

Our coaching staff, medical team, academic personnel, and strength coaches were all knowledgeable and professional, so there was little tangible disagreement or strife. Yet there also wasn't the willingness to sacrifice for each other or the players that often set great organizations apart from good ones.

We developed a relationship with Omaha sports psychologist Jack Stark about that time. I told Jack that I was unhappy with the general cohesiveness of our organization and felt that we needed to make an extensive assessment of the situation. Jack came up with the idea of instituting an accountability group, known as the "Unity Council." He recommended that each segment of the football team elect two representatives to a council that would meet weekly. Two defensive linemen, defensive ends, linebackers, running backs, defensive backs, quarterbacks, kickers, receivers, and offensive linemen were elected to the Council.

In all, 18 players were chosen as representatives of the football team. In their weekly meetings, the players addressed issues they felt were contributing to a lack of team morale and unity. Often, those players were unwilling to approach the coaching staff with their concerns but would discuss issues that were bothering them with their teammates on the Unity Council.

Many relatively minor issues surfaced, but those concerns, no matter how trivial, irritated the players and resulted in disruption on the team. A wide range of concerns were presented to the Unity Council. Issues such as location of the television sets in the dressing room, difficulty with getting shoes that fit properly, dissatisfaction with the selection of a Friday-night movie, the type of music being played in the weight room, and so on were presented.

Each week the Unity Council brought issues to the coaching staff, which were then further discussed and resolved in a full team meeting. There was little that could be done, however, about some complaints. For example, some players wanted to wear a different brand of football shoe. It was impossible to get all 150 players to like the same shoe. We explained that we could contract with only one shoe company and that we had chosen the company that seemed to satisfy the largest number of players. Getting the issue out in the open and discussing it seemed to quiet most concerns.

There ended up being few complaints that could not be resolved. In most cases, once the problem was brought to our attention, it was very easy to take the steps necessary to rectify the situation. Addressing these issues, no matter how minor, improved team morale almost immediately, as the players felt their opinions mattered and would be taken seriously.

Team discipline was another area that needed to be addressed. Sometimes players felt that one player was given disciplinary preference over another. This was usually a misperception, as the players did not know the history or background of every disciplinary episode. As Joe Paterno, longtime football coach at Penn State, once said in a meeting that I attended, "It is important not only to be fair; it is also important to appear to be fair." The Unity Council provided a forum where concerns about discipline could be openly discussed.

The Unity Council developed a uniform point system whereby

each player infraction resulted in an assessment of points. The table below lists the points assessed for each rule violation.

Points Violation

5 Felony Conviction
4 Drug Policy Violation
4 Misdemeanor Civil Offense Conviction
4 Academic Dishonesty
3 Unexcused Absence from Football Practice
2 Unexcused Absence from Team Meeting
2 Unexcused Absence from Unity Council Meeting
1 Unexcused Absence from Conditioning Session
1 Unexcused Absence from Scheduled Class
1 Unexcused Absence from Assigned Study Hall
1 Unexcused Absence from Appointment with Tutor
1 Failure to Follow Instructions

The disciplinary code was helpful, as it enabled each athlete to know and understand exactly what the consequences of his actions would be. The most serious infraction was a felony conviction, which resulted in the assessment of five points. Anytime a player was assessed a total of five points, suspension was automatic and the Unity Council made a recommendation concerning the length of suspension. The head coach had final authority in determining the disposition of each case; however, the Unity Council recommendation was weighed heavily. In serious matters, such as conviction of a felony, the suspension would normally be permanent.

Any combination of points resulting in a total of five points or more resulted in suspension. A player might receive five points for missing five classes. If he missed a team meeting (two points) and a practice (three points), he would be suspended. Noncriminal behavior resulting in a five-point total normally resulted in a single-game suspension. If illegal behavior was involved, the suspension was longer or even permanent.

A wide range of misbehavior resulted in one-point violations that added up quickly if a player was not properly focused. Codifying the infractions and giving them an assigned point total resulted in a clearer understanding of the consequences of undesirable behavior.

A list of procedures was drawn up by the Unity Council describing how points were to be assigned and what recourse a player would have if he believed that points were unjustly assigned. Enforcement procedures were as follows:

Enforcement

Athlete is notified of point(s).

Athlete can first attempt to resolve dispute with the person who issued the point.

Athlete can go before the Unity Council at their next scheduled meeting to dispute any point(s).

Accumulation of three points = a meeting with the Unity Council.

Three appearances before Unity Council in one year = suspension.

Accumulation of four points = parents contacted by Coach Osborne, player meets with Coach Osborne.

Accumulation of five points = Unity Council recommendation that the player is held out of a football game in fall semester and loses complimentary game tickets, or misses one week of spring practice and the spring game in the spring semester, or is suspended from program.

In the event an action is not covered by the existing point system, the head coach will determine appropriate action to be taken.

This procedural chart ensured that players understood the point system and how it would be enforced. Once a player accumulated three points, he was required to appear before the Unity Council to explain why he had received the points. At that time, the Unity Council members would discuss with the player what might be done to improve his behavior, as well as how he could be a better team member. A player receiving four points was required to meet with the Unity Council and the head coach. The player's parents were also notified that he was in danger of being suspended from the football team. Upon receiving five points, a player was suspended, but not until he appeared before the Unity Council and met with the head football coach. He was given a chance to appeal his case one final time.

A dispute over an assigned point was taken up with the coach, academic counselor, or strength staff member who assigned the point. For example, an academic counselor might check a class and not see the athlete present, resulting in a point being assessed. Sometimes the player would maintain that he was present in the class. If others in the class or the professor could vouch for his attendance, the point was removed. No system is perfect, and there were times that the Unity Council had to decide whether or not a point would stand when conflicting evidence was presented. The system was fair, however, in that everyone had a chance to speak his piece and no one felt railroaded into an unfair decision.

We also believed it was important to reward positive behavior. If a player who had previously received points did everything properly for one week, a point was taken away. Therefore, a player with four points who went two weeks in a row without receiving any additional points could reduce his total to two points. If there were no way to reward good behavior and the points stood for the duration of the school year, we would eventually have had a large number of suspended players.

The system was stringent. The average student at the university did not routinely have classes checked, undergo drug tests, and have his or her activities screened daily by the press for inappropriate behavior. But the average student did not receive as much attention on Saturday afternoons in the fall, either. Life in the public eye is not without a price.

The system worked well. The most positive feature of the point system was that it eliminated the perception of unequal treatment among players. For example, before the point system was installed, a player who was guilty of the violation known as minor in possession of alcohol might be dismissed from the team. Another player, found guilty of the same violation, would be suspended for one football game. Most players would not know that the player who was dismissed from the team had been in trouble previously and had been warned that more trouble would result in his dismissal. The player who was suspended for one football game was a first offender who had only the one violation of team policy the whole time he had been on the team.

So players were called before the Unity Council and points were reviewed, and it was not long before the Unity Council members, and the majority of the football team, began to realize which players were consistently out of line and which players were doing the right things.

Since it was against policy to disclose drug test results, a person who received four points for failing a drug test would appear before the Unity Council without any specific allegation made against him. It was not long before the Unity Council members began to get a good idea of why these individuals were called before the Unity Council. The Unity Council would deal with each case based on the number of points accumulated.

We had a few cases involving drug abuse. When a player failed a drug test, his parents were notified, and he was evaluated by a substance-abuse counselor. He was then given a weekly drug test to ensure that there was no further usage.

During my coaching career at Nebraska, we saw practically no cocaine abuse and little steroid use. Marijuana and alcohol had to be dealt with more frequently. On occasion, a player who tested positive for marijuana proved to be a habitual user who had been using since age 12 or 13. The prognosis for these players was never good. Try as we might, with weekly drug tests and individual and group therapy, these young men would usually go back to their habit when they encountered some personal difficulty. They would often straighten up for a few weeks or months, but marijuana exerted its powerful hold when life became difficult. Most of these players failed three drug tests and were dismissed from the football program within a year. It was surprising how these players could use marijuana from middle-school years through high school and still be well recommended by their coaches and teachers. Although we would not recruit someone with a known drug problem, we seemed to get one or two surprises each year.

One of those surprises involved a recruit from Nebraska who had signed a letter of intent with us. A few weeks later, we heard rumors of the young man's possible involvement with drugs. We confronted him with these rumors and expressed our concerns about him. He told us he had used marijuana only once and that had been several months previously. He was adamant that he did not use drugs, that his one-time use was an isolated event. At that point, we asked him if he would be willing to take a drug test. We assumed that if he was using marijuana he would test positive, since marijuana usage is usually detectable for three to four weeks afterward. The young man agreed to the test. The results indicated that he had not been using drugs, and we decided to still honor his scholarship.

When he reported for football practice the next August and took his physical examination, we found that he was positive on the marijuana test. Despite various intervention efforts throughout the remainder of the school year, including individual counseling, group therapy, and weekly testing, he tested positive for a second and third time and was dismissed from the team.

Our policy entailed permanent dismissal after three positive drug tests. More often than not, players who had been heavily involved with marijuana or other drugs at an early age struggled not to revert back to their old habits when they were under stress. We had a very strong support system, but with cases involving such a long-standing history of drug use, even that support system was often not enough.

I was proud that we never had a player arrested for selling or using drugs. We avoided any major drug scandal, and any usage we did see was relatively infrequent. I attribute this low drug-abuse rate at least partially to the fact that we regularly tested our players for drugs and continually educated and warned them about the problems of drug abuse. We drug-tested players who were on our campus in the summer. Most teams do not drug-test during the summer months. However, we recognized that summer provides a three-month window where some athletes have a temptation to use either recreational or performance-enhancing drugs because they believe that such usage will go undetected at that time of year. We didn't ever allow the players to feel that there was a "safe" period during the year in which drug testing would not occur.

The disciplinary code implemented by the Unity Council led to an internal discipline, one that was not imposed by the coaching staff. Peer pressure became a positive factor rather than a negative. If a player was out of line, other players would encourage him to straighten up. Sometimes an appearance before the Unity Council was so distressing that a player would break down in tears. Admitting to fellow players behavior that contradicted team policy was often harder than being confronted by coaches. Jack Stark mentioned one such occasion in 1993. Trev Alberts, one of our captains and a Unity Council member, went to the room of a player who was devastated by his appearance before the Unity Council. Trev spent time comforting the player, as the Unity Council was interested in changing negative behavior, not creating an emotional crisis.

Professional basketball coach Pat Riley refers to the use of peer influence in discussing what he calls the "Core Covenant":

> The essence of the Core Covenant is totally positive peer pressure. It replaces blaming and finger-pointing—two vicious enemies of teamwork—with mutual monitoring and mutual reinforcement. . . . Positive peer pressure intensifies any team's performance and brings it closer to peak.

We occasionally had a player involved in an alcohol-related incident. Alcohol is a drug and was treated as a drug when Unity Council points were assessed. Minor in possession, public intoxication, and alcohol detected in a drug test were all classified as four-point violations. Since alcohol is water soluble, it leaves the system quickly. Therefore, if we suspected a player had a drinking problem, we tested him early in the morning. If he had used alcohol the night before, it would be detected, and he would be in violation of our drug code.

I became convinced that a college team that abstained from alcohol use would have a decided edge over their competition. Alcohol abuse is so prevalent on the college campus that most athletes are influenced by a binge-drinking culture. Therefore, I talked extensively to the players about the consequences of alcohol abuse. I first explained how practice and game performance were affected by alcohol abuse. The effects of heavy drinking affected performance for several days. Second, I pointed out that most of the negative behavior that drew public attention to athletes is either directly or indirectly alcohol-related. During my time as head football coach, more than 90 percent of the serious incidents that we dealt with at Nebraska were related to alcohol.

During the five-year run from 1993 through 1997, in which we were 60–3, our squads voted to abstain from using alcohol during the season. Abstinence from alcohol was a team policy and was enforced internally. I am certain that the great majority of players adhered to the policy, and it made a difference. Alcohol is a depressant, lessens physical strength, and interferes with normal sleep patterns. It seems strange to say that an athletic team abstaining from alcohol is an anomaly, yet in our present culture I believe that it is.

The Unity Council disciplinary system was not without its difficulties. A major problem occurred when a player was charged with criminal activity by authorities. In these cases, there was immediate media attention. However, the final disposition of the case in the courts often did not take place for several weeks, months, or even years. Team policy clearly stated that a player was not to be disciplined because he was charged with a felony or misdemeanor. He had to be convicted of the crime he was charged with before disciplinary action was taken.

Christian Peter's case was very difficult for me personally. Disturbing allegations of sexual assault and rape continued to surface. Christian's version of the story was quite different from that of the young woman accusing him, and the controversy continued to swirl. The alleged rape was thoroughly investigated by law-enforcement officials and no evidence of wrongdoing was found.

The allegations against Christian were so widely publicized that he was actually "undrafted" by the New England Patriots. The day after the NFL draft ended, they decided to remove him from their draft list. He had been drafted in the fifth round, but the owner of the Patriots later informed me that they were unaware of Christian's past when they drafted him. This was pure nonsense, as I had talked to people in professional football who assured me that everyone had a complete history of Christian's background, including the Patriots.

I liked Christian. He was a very hard worker and was committed to the team. Christian was not without his faults, however. He has been the object of more accusations and negative press than almost anyone I have known. Yet he has refused to go public with his side of the story. I hope that with time and effort, his reputation can be restored.

My faith leads me to look at what a person is capable of becoming and not just at his misdeeds. Often, the player responds to this vision of what he could be. So far, I have been encouraged by the direction Christian's life has taken after leaving Nebraska. Christian has quit drinking, has taken an active part in running his family's New Jersey restaurant, and has become a productive defensive lineman for the New York Giants.

There were times when it appeared that charges were not accurate. One such case, discussed previously, was that involving Riley Washington. Riley's case was complicated by a year and a half of court delays from when he was first charged until it was finally decided by a jury. Because of the publicity surrounding the case, many people believed that he was guilty, yet the evidence indicated otherwise. We did not dismiss him from the team, because he had not been convicted of any crime and all of the evidence presented to us indicated his innocence. Remaining true to the tenets of our disciplinary code was difficult because of the lengthy legal process. There was some vindication when he was cleared of all charges.

Lawrence Phillips was charged with two misdemeanors: (1) for illegally entering the apartment where he found his former girlfriend and (2) for pulling her down three flights of stairs. He entered a plea of no contest, an admission of guilt. Each misdemeanor was worth four points on the Unity Council scale, so Lawrence accumulated eight points. He had also failed to follow instructions and had missed class, bringing his point total to ten. According to the disciplinary code, Lawrence was to be held out of at least two games. The Unity Council and most of the players agreed that a suspension was in order; however, they did not believe that permanent suspension was warranted.

When media coverage was involved, things became very difficult. It was important to get as many facts as possible and not rush to judgment, yet newspaper and television reporters wanted statements immediately. I was often asked to comment on alleged misbehavior before I knew what the charges were or had talked to the player. I agonized over each case involving a player, as I realized that what was decided would have a great impact on that player's life and the football team, as well. The player and the team were my main concerns.

There was often tension between what was best for the individual and what might be best for the team as a whole. In Lawrence Phillips's case, for example, it appeared the best thing for Lawrence was to stay on the team. This seemed to coincide with what the majority of players on the team felt was the right thing to do, so the decision was not terribly difficult to make. I was not necessarily unconcerned about the media or public perception, but I knew that if decisions were based on the opinions of those outside the program, who often knew very little about the particulars of each case, we would end up with a chaotic situation. My faith told me that every player was of great worth irrespective of his athletic talent, and I could not, in good conscience, throw someone away to lessen public criticism.

I believed that Lawrence needed a thorough evaluation before any final decision concerning his future was made. Jack Stark arranged this testing at the Menninger Clinic in Topeka, Kansas. The evaluation did not reveal any major psychiatric problem. Following his evaluation, Lawrence was required to meet academic responsibilities and attend counseling. I knew that the only thing that would keep Lawrence on track was the possibility of playing football again. He loved football and seemed to need that structure and discipline in his life. Lawrence was off the team for six weeks and was kept out of a starting role for two more weeks. While most players felt that Lawrence deserved some serious penalty, many thought that the suspension was longer than the point system required and would have been upset had Lawrence been permanently dismissed from the team.

I spent time examining each disciplinary case in a spiritual sense and subjected each situation to prayer. Even today, I'm not sure I made the right decision in regard to Lawrence Phillips. He has done little to this point to indicate that he is willing to make changes after having been given another chance. I thought Lawrence had done very well in his rehabilitation and counseling during the four months he stayed in Nebraska after the assault. In January, following our bowl game with Florida, I spoke to Lawrence's agent. I told the agent that Lawrence needed continual counseling and a great deal of structure. I felt reasonably good about Lawrence's chances of getting his life in order if this was done. Unfortunately, there was a four-month period between Lawrence's leaving Lincoln and the NFL draft. Lawrence went back to California and started hanging out with some of his former friends from the group home. He bought a car and began to entertain his friends. He had little structure in his life and things went downhill in a hurry. Before long, Lawrence was picked up for driving under the influence of alcohol. At that point, it seemed that the progress he had made in the four months of rehabilitation at Nebraska had evaporated. However, Lawrence set a league rushing record with Barcelona of NFL Europe in the spring of 1999. Hopefully this is a sign of better things to come.

It was difficult to explain the Unity Council disciplinary code to the media. Any such explanation would be seen as a cop-out. As a result, the coaching staff and I took a hammering from the national media. The most important thing, however, was that the football team understood what Lawrence had done and what the policy was, and felt that the matter had been handled fairly.

Tyrone Williams's case also presented difficulties. He was accused of firing a .22 revolver and striking the trunk of an occupied automobile. Even though there was no evidence he was trying to hit the car's occupants, he was charged with two felonies. His attorneys strongly disagreed with the charges against him. They believed that the two felony charges were for essentially the same thing, resulting in double jeopardy. Since his case was not decided until long after his playing career was over, I disciplined Tyrone for what I knew he had done and admitted to, but I did not dismiss him from the team.

There is a common belief that athletes are more likely to engage in violence than nonathletes. Studies using extremely small samples or questionable research methodology are often cited as "proof." Richard Lapchick, director of Northeastern University's Center for the Study of Sport in Society, disagrees with this "data." Richard refers to statistics indicating that 3 million women were victims of battering in 1995. That same year, 72 athletes and 7 coaches were accused of gender violence. Since a total of 212,000 men play or coach a college or pro sport, this means that approximately 1 out of every 3,000 athletes or coaches was implicated. This data indicates that athletes are actually less likely to be involved in assaulting women than are those in the general population. One assault by an athlete is too many. I am not excusing violence. It does seem, however, that some common perceptions of athletes and violence may not be accurate.

My experience has been that an athlete is often accused because of his greater visibility. A case in point is that of Grant Wistrom, an All-American defensive end for us in 1997. Shortly after completing his career, Grant witnessed another young man treating a young woman badly. Grant stepped in and was struck in the eye and suffered a black eye and a cut lip. The initial reports were that Grant had assaulted the young man, when actually Grant did not retaliate and simply walked away knowing that any retaliation would reflect negatively on the team and on Grant. Because of his visibility as an athlete, however, Grant was singled out as the aggressor, even though this was totally untrue.

There may have been flaws in the disciplinary code, as it is hard to devise a single code that covers a wide variety of behaviors. However, we wanted a system that was relatively simple and easily understood by everyone involved. We did not want to have the Unity Council code turn into a complicated and burdensome legal document. Since we had to satisfy federal and state laws, conference rules, University of Nebraska regulations, and Unity Council standards—all under the glare of media scrutiny—we were often placed in difficult situations.

Some of our players came from situations where the basic tenets of the code of conduct were not commonly practiced. Being on time, not missing class, and avoiding brushes with the law were not values they had grown up with. The Unity Council, themes of the week, and a steady emphasis on character development began to create a common team value system. I noticed a steady improvement in attitude and team chemistry.

We not only worked hard on unity issues with the players, we also spent a great deal of time strengthening cohesion with the coaching staff, strength coaches, trainers, academic counselors, and equipment managers. Every member of the athletic department who had an impact on football players in some way was made aware of our focus on unity. We held meetings attended by everyone involved with the football team in which we discussed how players were to be treated, as well as the importance of maintaining a unified front. Occasionally, someone on the medical staff would question something that was going on in the strength program. A coach might be concerned about a procedure in the training room, or an academic counselor might be critical of a coach. Divisive comments and turf battles were discouraged by Jack Stark and me. Instead, great efforts were made to ensure that all of the individuals who had any impact on the players were positive toward the players and other staff members.

It was particularly important that the football coaches were totally unified. There is often bickering within a coaching staff. This division is picked up quickly by the players. No negativism on the part of one coach toward another was tolerated, and we emphasized this need for unity on a regular basis in our staff meetings. If there was a problem, we got it out in the open and discussed it as a staff.

Boyd Epley, our strength coach, posted signs emphasizing unity in our meeting rooms. He met with the Unity Council, along with our sports psychologist, Jack Stark, on a weekly basis. Dennis LeBlanc, the director of Academic Support Services, often met with the Unity Council to answer any questions related to points assessed for violations of class attendance or study hall policies. Occasionally, one of the football coaches met with the Unity Council to make sure that the Council representatives got better acquainted with the coaching staff. The Unity Council had opportunities to talk directly with each coach and express any concern about how that coach treated players or conducted his drills and practices.

If there were concerns about athletic department policies, the athletic director met with the Unity Council. If there were issues about equipment, the equipment manager would meet with them. Anytime there were matters that I needed to discuss with them as head coach, I would attend the Unity Council meeting myself.

As time went on, I began to see that our focus on unity had four major positive consequences for our team:

1. The Unity Council empowered the players. They began to see that their concerns were heard and addressed. I read the list

of concerns brought up in the Unity Council and addressed those concerns in the team meeting the next day. When the players felt that they were being heard, team morale improved.

2. The players developed a better understanding of what was considered acceptable and unacceptable behavior, as well as what the consequences of inappropriate behavior would be. They believed that the system was fair and applied equally to everyone.

3. Players began to accept responsibility for team standards. Rules were not imposed from the top down so much as they were enforced from the bottom up. Players were more aware than the coaches of off-field activity that was damaging to the team, and they addressed that behavior before it escalated into a major news event. We saw the players begin to take ownership of team standards.

4. Unity among players, coaches, and support staff became more prevalent. Complaints in the locker room decreased. Dissension was rare. Everyone was committed to a common mission. Whether we won or not, the unity, mutual concern, and caring were palpable and made the journey much more enjoyable.

It is dangerous to generalize too broadly in examining cause and effect. To say that the Unity Council was solely responsible for improved performance is too simplistic. There is no question, however, that it contributed to an improved attitude, which, in turn, translated into success on the field.

After the Unity Council was initiated, we won seven consecutive conference or divisional titles and three national championships. I am convinced that exceptional team chemistry was a key factor in this stretch, and that the Unity Council played a significant part in developing this chemistry.

8

Hanging in There

Great works are performed not by strength
but by perseverance.
—Samuel Johnson

At the beginning of each season at Nebraska, we assembled the incoming freshmen players and discussed some of the challenges they would be facing during their college careers. They would be away from home for the first time, would be challenged athletically and academically as they had never been before, and would receive more media attention than they had previously experienced. I asked them to look around the room and take note of each player sitting there. I explained to them that if they did the same thing two or three years later, they would be surprised to see who was still there and who wasn't.

Traditionally, Nebraska University football has had a relatively low attrition rate; however, almost every program will lose some players. I told the players that the factor determining who would still be around two years later would not be the number of scholarship offers they had received. Several of these young men could have gone to any school in the country, having received as many as 40 or 50 scholarship offers. Some had only one or two scholarship offers. Nearly half of them were walk-ons who had no Division I scholarship opportunities. I also explained that their longevity would not be determined by physical ability, as almost everyone in the room had enough ability to eventually mature into a solid player. The single most important factor determining who would still be playing at Nebraska two or three years later was perseverance.

Perseverance, both on and off the field, is a quality to which I attributed the successful careers of many Nebraska players. The player who attended class and went to practice, despite being homesick or discouraged; the player who was injured and worked hard every day with the trainers to rehabilitate his injury; the player who had a bad season yet rededicated himself and worked hard in the off-season, would ultimately be successful. Sometimes I shared the story of Abraham Lincoln with the freshmen. I explained how Lincoln exemplified success through persever- ance. Despite several business failures and losing every election early in his political career, he persevered and became one of the greatest presidents in United States history.

I witnessed firsthand the importance of perseverance upon entering professional football. I was drafted by the San Francisco 49ers in the eighteenth round of the NFL draft in the spring of 1959. Currently, the NFL draft lasts through only seven rounds, but at that time, there were no more than a dozen NFL teams, so the talent pool was deeper and the draft lasted 20 rounds.

Being the eighteenth draft pick and coming from a small col- lege like Hastings College did not enhance my chances of mak- ing the San Francisco 49ers. Neither did the fact that 90 players reported to training camp, with only 36 spots available on the playing roster and 36 veterans returning. Usually the top two or three draft picks automatically make the team, so there was prac- tically no room for someone drafted in the late rounds. To make matters worse, on the first day of camp, the head coach informed me that they had two excellent, experienced quarterbacks, John Brodie and Y. A. Tittle, and that they were going to keep only two quarterbacks on the roster. Since I had been a quarterback in high school and college, Coach Red Hickey told me that if I felt I could beat one of those two quarterbacks out, I should go ahead and try. Otherwise, I would be better off to try another position. It didn't take me long to figure out that a position change was in order. I decided to pursue the unfamiliar position of receiver. Inexperienced, I took it one day at a time and did the best I could to learn the new position. Despite astronomical odds against my hanging around, one player after another eliminated himself. I recall having the 49ers' number-one draft pick ask me to give him a ride to the bus station. He was homesick and left without notifying the coaches.

Our training camp was held at tiny St. Mary's College, located in the countryside east of Oakland. Two-a-day practices lasted for six weeks, the temperature was often near 100 degrees, and competition was intense. Eventually, I was able to hang on as a member of the "taxi squad," a five-man unit carried over and above the regular playing roster that was used for practice purposes and could be called upon if there was an injury. Former congressman Jack Kemp and I were both on the taxi squad. We got to know each other quite well and roomed together on road trips.

Persevering through the challenges of my first year in the NFL eventually paid off. I was picked up by the Washington Redskins the next year and was able to play in the 1960 and 1961 seasons. In 1961, I started as a flanker for the Redskins. I was unable to return for the 1962 season due to a hamstring injury sustained in the 1961 season. The whole episode taught me, however, that perseverance and staying power would often pay dividends. The only sure way to fail was to quit.

Two players who displayed exceptional perseverance enrolled at the University of Nebraska in the fall of 1992. John Hesse was a heavily recruited player from Lincoln, Nebraska. He had good size and was an excellent high school athlete, excelling at several positions. Matt Turman was a walk-on player from Wahoo, Nebraska. Although not very big, Matt was a talented high school athlete. He had played quarterback in high school, but we felt he would be a better college player as a receiver or defensive back because of his relatively small stature. Both John and Matt "redshirted" their first year. Neither of them was in position to play a significant amount, so we held them out of competition, as we do almost any freshman player in that circumstance.

A redshirt year is discouraging and difficult for a player. Not only is there a lot to learn about football, but the player is making personal and social adjustments to college life, as well. Most of the time, a redshirt player is placed on the scout team, simulating the upcoming opponent and getting knocked around by the players on the top units. Redshirting as a freshman, however, is tolerable if the player gets to play in his second year. We had trouble finding a position for John and Matt to play, so they remained on the scout team for yet another year.

John played different positions and couldn't seem to find his niche. He grew frustrated as this pattern continued into his third year, although he did play some on the kicking teams. In his fourth year, as a redshirt junior, he began to play some as a linebacker, but still wasn't playing as much as he had hoped. I sensed John's discouragement. He came to see me about twice a year, expressing his frustration over not playing and to see if there was anything he could do to improve. However, John never became so discouraged that he gave up.

John was intelligent and kept learning, adjusting, and getting better. He worked very hard during the off-season to improve his quickness and agility. Eventually, John found his niche and settled in at middle linebacker. In his senior year, John got his opportunity to show what he could do and blossomed into a great player. He not only started but, in my estimation, was the best middle linebacker in the Big 12 Conference. His willingness to persevere was a critical component of his success. John played well enough his senior year to be drafted into the NFL, eventually playing for the world champion Denver Broncos and later with the St. Louis Rams.

John's case was typical of many highly recruited players. These young men often expected big things and later found that there were many other outstanding players on the team. Playing time was hard to come by. Some heavily recruited players gave up when things did not come easily for them. Others, like John, would hang in there despite their disappointment. Most of these young men who persevered ultimately made a significant contribution to our football team.

Matt Turman was not recruited by any major university and appeared to be a long shot when he enrolled at Nebraska. He had a big heart, but he was not as large or as talented as many other players. Matt redshirted his first year and played very little the next year, spending a second season on the scouting team. He bounced from position to position, and finally, due to several injuries at the quarterback spot, was moved back to quarterback. Matt stepped in and started a critical game at Kansas State in 1994 when Tommie Frazier and Brook Berringer, our top two quarterbacks, were both down with injuries. Matt played a crucial role in the game and helped us preserve an undefeated season. The Kansas State game was the only time Matt started at

Nebraska; however, his experience, knowledge of the offense, and competitive spirit enabled him to play a key role for us as a backup quarterback for the next two years. During his first two years, it was questionable whether Matt would be able to play at a Division I level. I'm sure the thought of transferring to a smaller school crossed his mind many times, but his extraordinary tenacity and perseverance influenced him to stay. Matt will be long remembered by Nebraska fans for the contribution he made and the exceptional courage he displayed.

Perseverance is an important quality. On more than one occasion I recall players saying, "If you stay, you play." The idea that "staying the course" would eventually pay off motivated many young players who did not get playing time early in their careers.

Perseverance was not important to the players alone; it was important to everyone involved with the football program. During the early part of my coaching career, we encountered some difficult times against the University of Oklahoma. We lost to them five straight years, from 1973 through 1977. Nebraska fans were not happy. Each of those years we lost the "big game" to Oklahoma and usually the Big 8 championship in the process. No one gave up, however. We kept working to get to the point where we were better than Oklahoma. In a sense, rather than being our enemy, Oklahoma became our ally. This team showed us our weaknesses and challenged us to strive for a higher standard. Albert Einstein sensed the importance and value that adversity can play when he said, "Out of clutter, find simplicity; from discord, find harmony. In the middle of difficulty lies opportunity."

The most difficult loss to Oklahoma was in 1973. It was my first Nebraska–Oklahoma game as head coach. We did not play well and lost the game 27–0 in Norman. We accomplished absolutely nothing on offense, never advancing the football across the 50-yard line, and had a hard time slowing Oklahoma down on defense. At that time, bowl selections were made prior to the final game of the season. The week before we played Oklahoma, we had been selected to play the Southwest Conference Champion, the University of Texas, in the Cotton Bowl.

Oklahoma was ineligible to go to a bowl game that year because they were on probation. So the Nebraska game at the end of the season was essentially their bowl game, and they played like it was. I still remember Field Scovell, chairman of the 1974 Cotton Bowl Committee, addressing the press after the Oklahoma game. Being the gentleman he was, Field tried to present the situation as best he could. He commented that this game didn't shine the Cotton Bowl up very much but that they were still pleased to have Nebraska in the Cotton Bowl playing Texas. I could tell by his long face that he would much rather have had any one of a dozen teams besides Nebraska at that point.

We went back to Lincoln licking our wounds and were in a rather poor state of mind as a team. We had won eight, lost two, and tied one. It was not bad for some programs, but it wasn't very good at Nebraska. Our fans still remembered the standard set by the 1970 and 1971 national championship teams. I responded to the situation by telling the players that we were going to work harder and improve as a team. Our goal was to beat Texas in the Cotton Bowl, and we were going to pay whatever price was necessary to prove that we were good enough to deserve the opportunity to play in a major bowl game. The only way to salvage the season, in my mind, was to beat Texas.

It wasn't long before the players held a players-only meeting. Some of the senior leaders on the team told the squad they were unhappy with the situation. They believed a bowl game should be a reward for a good season. They wanted to have a good time at the bowl and didn't think it was right to have to work as hard as the coaching staff required. This was the first crisis I had to face as a head coach. I responded by suspending one of our team captains. This individual had been most vocal about not working hard in bowl preparation and had called the players-only meeting. I believed that his role as captain required that he approach the coaching staff with his concerns before he called a meeting with the players. I wasn't sure how the team would respond to my decision to suspend the talented and popular captain. There could have been a mutiny. Fortunately, however, everyone stayed in harness, and we began to work extraordinarily hard for the game. Eventually, the suspended team captain came in and apologized. We reinstated him on the team, and he played very well in the Cotton Bowl.

Despite being heavy underdogs in the game, we beat Texas 19–3 and managed to salvage a decent season. I'm sure that had we lost the bowl game, as most people thought we would, the wolves really would have been out in force. A loss would have left us with an 8–3–1 season, definitely not acceptable in Nebraska.

Often, the ability to persevere depends on how one deals with adversity. Adversity befalls every individual and organization from time to time. The most important factor in overcoming adversity is to remain positive. When things don't go well there is often a tendency for coaches to get down on players. Players also begin looking for someone else to blame and point the finger at the coaches or each other. The whole situation often quickly disintegrates. After the poor performance at Oklahoma in 1973, we did not dwell on the loss. Instead of casting the blame, we focused immediately on working hard. A commitment to effort and discipline became critical; it took the players' minds off negative factors and kept them focused on something positive—improvement.

It was at this time that I realized how helpful Oklahoma was to us. Oklahoma was a team we were expected to beat, and through those years of frustration and disappointment we learned some valuable lessons. One of those lessons had to do with competing in a constructive rather than destructive way. When another team has great success in beating your team, there is often a tendency to want to try to pull the other team down to your level. Sometimes this is done by disparaging the competitor in recruiting. Every negative bit of information concerning the competition is dredged up and relayed to the recruit and his parents. In some cases, such information is nothing more than unfounded hearsay. Furthermore, if there is any hint of impropriety in regard to NCAA rules, it is not uncommon for competing schools to turn each other in for violations.

Our approach was to raise our own level of play to that of Oklahoma. We studied every team who had had success against Oklahoma and evaluated our program in great detail to assess what we needed to do to perform at Oklahoma's level. There is no question that our focus on improvement made us a better team. We eventually got to the place where we felt that we could compete on an even footing with any team in the country. Games involving Michigan and Ohio State, Texas and Texas A&M, UCLA and USC, Alabama and Auburn, and Florida and Florida State are intense because the schools are in geographical proximity. They recruit the same players and their fans live next door to each other. Sometimes the competition gets heated and ugly. Oklahoma was the team we needed to beat in the 1960s, 1970s, and 1980s, yet they were located 400 miles away and we seldom competed for the same recruits. As a result, the competition was healthy and seldom got out of hand. The Oklahoma coach, Barry Switzer, and I got along well and both schools benefited from the competition.

We tried to look at each loss as a learning opportunity as well as a chance to get better. One of the things we learned was how to defense the wishbone. At that time, Oklahoma ran the wishbone offense better than any team in the nation. Few teams ran the wishbone, so we saw it only once or twice a season.

The first few times we played the wishbone, we didn't do a good job of stopping it. We made major defensive changes in those games against Oklahoma. We scrapped our basic defensive alignment and played a defensive scheme they had not seen before. We did this to confuse the wishbone quarterback reads and their blocking assignments. The problem with this strategy was that, even though it caused confusion for Oklahoma early in the game, they would eventually adjust. Their offensive coordinator, Galen Hall, was sharp and we were easily dismantled as the game went on. Eventually, we realized that we needed to stay with the basic defensive scheme we had used throughout the season. We adjusted our standard defense to the wishbone through repetition against their best plays and quit making major defensive changes. We began to hang in there better on defense. The games no longer looked like a track meet, with Oklahoma doing most of the running.

As our games against Oklahoma became closer, the deciding factor was often the athletic ability of their quarterback. On several occasions, we had Oklahoma in trouble late in the game, and their quarterback, through speed and athleticism, would make a key play. He would scramble on a pass play or would run an option and would turn a bad situation into a first down or a touchdown. I began to realize that we would not be able to beat Oklahoma with any consistency unless we started to match their athleticism at quarterback. We began to recruit quarterbacks who were not just outstanding passers but could scramble, run the option, and had the ability to make great individual plays through speed and agility. We finally beat Oklahoma in 1978, and we began to beat them with greater regularity in the 1980s. Our sounder defensive philosophy and greater speed at quarterback began to pay off, not only against Oklahoma but against other teams, as well.

We survived our struggles with Oklahoma only to face more adversity in bowl games. Starting with the 1987 Fiesta Bowl against Florida State, we lost seven straight bowl games. It appeared that we had the Fiesta Bowl game against Florida State won. We were about to put the game away with a final touchdown late in the game and then fumbled at the Florida State one-yard line. The Seminoles proceeded to drive the length of the field to win the game in the final minute. This started us on a slide in bowl games that was hard to understand.

Losing a bowl game is always difficult because it is the final game. Losing the last game of the season means you have to live with that loss for the next seven months. The fans didn't forget it, and our players and coaches didn't forget either. Many bowl games were played against southern teams on their home field. I often wished that we could have played Florida State or Miami on New Year's Day in Lincoln, Nebraska, as I thought that our odds would improve considerably. However, we usually ended up playing them in the Orange Bowl on a grass field. They were acclimated to grass fields and humidity, whereas we played our late-season games in very cold weather with low humidity on artificial turf. Making excuses was not helpful, however. We simply needed to perform at a level where we were good enough to beat those teams, regardless of the location and playing conditions.

Two of our seven bowl losses were to the University of Miami in the Orange Bowl, two losses were to Florida State in the Orange Bowl, and one loss was to Florida State in the Fiesta Bowl. Both Florida State and Miami had great speed and played a 4–3 defensive alignment. The 4–3 defense allowed them to make defensive adjustments very quickly and also enabled them to generate a great pass rush. After evaluating our situation, we decided to change our defensive alignment from a 5–2 to a 4–3 spacing. We not only changed our alignment, we also altered our defensive philosophy. We had been a reading defense, reacting to what the offense did. We changed to an attacking defense. This allowed us to penetrate the line of scrimmage and disrupt the opposing offense. We were a more aggressive team. The players enjoyed the defensive change, and we elevated our level of play. We finally got to the place where we were able to beat the best teams in the nation on their home turf.

There was a continuous clamor from many sportswriters and fans for us to eliminate our heavy emphasis on the running game and adopt a passing attack like Miami and Florida State. As a coaching staff, however, we believed that our offensive philosophy was sound and were confident that we could beat teams like Florida State or Miami with the offensive attack we had been using. We ran the football three-fourths of the time, with option football being a basic part of our running game.

Offensively, we had to be good enough to get to the Orange Bowl, and this meant playing games in Nebraska, Kansas, Iowa, and Colorado in October and November. Some of those games were played in cold weather, accompanied by strong winds. A powerful running game in such weather was critical. Cold temperatures and strong winds are devastating to a passing game. We stayed with the offensive strategy we felt would be successful in the Big 8 Conference, assuming that if we made it to the bowl game enough times and recruited the right players, we would eventually win the key games.

Because of those bowl losses, we not only changed to a 4–3 defense, we also gained a better understanding of how to attack the 4–3 defense from an offensive standpoint. Throughout the regular season, we did not see a 4–3 defense very much. When we encountered the 4–3 in key bowl games, our blocking adjustments and play calling was not as effective as it might have been with more familiarity. We eventually developed an inside running game and some options that were effective against the 4–3 defense.

More emphasis was also placed on speed in recruiting. We noticed that the defensive speed of Florida State and Miami made it especially difficult for us to move the ball against them in our bowl games. Our improvement on defense, greater team speed, and improved knowledge of how to attack the 4–3 defense began to serve us well.

Following our seven consecutive bowl game losses, many fans and observers began to question our ability to win "the big one," particularly the national championship. Had we beaten Clemson in the 1982 Orange Bowl, we possibly could have been named national champions. If we had beaten Penn State during the 1982 season, we had an excellent chance to end the season on top. A victory over Miami in the 1984 Orange Bowl definitely would have given us a national championship. In the 1994 Orange Bowl, we narrowly lost to Florida State at the end of the game and again were thwarted in our attempt to win a national championship.

The Nebraska fans appreciated our ability in coming that close; however, the desire to win a national championship often outweighed appreciation of the effort we made in those near misses. As time went on, we acquired the reputation of being a very good team who couldn't get over the hump when the national championship was on the line.

Some of the difficulty in winning the national championship games may have been my fault. I believed that our goal should be to be the best team we were capable of being, and I was reluctant to encourage the players to set the national championship as their ultimate goal. I realized that if the players were focused on a national championship and they lost a game or two early in the season, their goal would already be unattainable, and I was afraid of the consequences. I have seen teams with lofty aspirations lose early games. When the chance of winning a championship was no longer possible because of early-season losses, these teams often lost their focus, unraveled, and had losing seasons.

As the years went by, I sensed the players' intense focus on the national championship. This was particularly true after the narrow 16–18 loss to Florida State at the conclusion of the 1993 season. At that point, the only thing left for our players was the national championship, and the 1994 season was dedicated to accomplishing that goal. We decided that the risk of an early loss or two and seeing our goal evaporate was one we would have to live with. It was a big motivational risk, as the odds against winning the national championship in any given year are great. Robert Louis Stevenson once said, "To be what we are, and to become what we are capable of becoming, is the only end of life." The players were ready to win a national championship, and we couldn't deny them the opportunity to become what they believed they were capable of becoming.

We proceeded to win national championships in 1994, 1995, and 1997. I attribute those titles to the outstanding competition we encountered in the bowl losses, as well as the focus and experience we acquired along the way.

Facing adversity in the bowl losses and losing national championship games served as a springboard to later success. It was all in our attitude. We were determined to learn from each loss and take something away from each disappointment that would later serve us well. Our team gradually improved to the point where we were not only capable of getting into national championship games, we were now capable of winning them. During the string of seven straight bowl losses, we lost to three teams who won the national championship. We knew firsthand what it took to win the whole thing.

Just as we learned something from playing top teams in big games, others benefited from playing against Nebraska. An *Arizona Republic* article, dated January 4, 1999, mentioned comments by Lawrence Wright, a former Florida defensive back, that Florida learned a great deal while playing Nebraska for the national championship following the 1995 season. He explained how Nebraska's strength and ability enabled Florida to gain insight into what it took to play at the top level. Florida used the Fiesta Bowl loss as a springboard to improve to the point where they won the national championship the next year.

In the same newspaper article, Tennessee wide receiver Peerless Price stated that playing Nebraska in the January 1998 Orange Bowl was a great help in their national championship season, which culminated in the 1999 Fiesta Bowl win over Florida State. He commented, "That game gave us a lot of knowledge of how strong big-time teams are. We had to get to that level." Another Tennessee player, Spencer Riley, said, "[Nebraska] had a different attitude about them than a lot of teams. They knew what they had to do. They had been there."

Prior to playing Arizona State in Tempe early in the 1996 season, we had won 26 straight games. We played poorly and lost to Arizona State 19–0. Many Nebraska fans were in shock. Some people thought our program was in major trouble. As coaches, we were as positive as possible with the players. We pointed out the good things that we did in the game. We played well on defense most of the time, had a good kicking game, and even had two or three good offensive series. We also emphasized how the loss could be helpful to us; we would learn a great deal from it and get better. We made several adjustments, particularly on offense, and ran off nine straight wins on the way to the north division Big 12 championship.

Benjamin Franklin once said, "The things which hurt, instruct." The loss to Arizona State was very instructional. We made adjustments not only on offense and defense, but also in our practice tempo, and we became a much better team.

Over time, I saw that the players who endured and persevered were ultimately successful. Many of them didn't get a great deal of playing time—some spent most of their careers on the scout team. However, they developed a tenacity that would serve them well throughout their lifetimes. Some of the most successful people in later life were players who learned how to "hang in there" under difficult circumstances. Many players have said that one of the real advantages they enjoyed in their business careers was the experience they gained on the athletic field. Some of those players did not appear to have profited a great deal from their athletic career while at Nebraska because they didn't play very much. In their minds, however, the experience was invaluable.

As an organization, we attempted to respond to adversity in a positive way. The bowl losses and the missed opportunities to win national championships, although very painful, served us well. We adjusted our defense, learned more about our offense, and changed our recruiting procedures. The distinguishing factor between success and failure is often the way we choose to respond to adversity. Confucius once said, "Our greatest glory is not in never falling, but in rising every time we fall." Woody Hayes, former Ohio State football coach, expressed this concept in football terminology when he said, "The lesson football teaches is that when you get knocked down, you get up and move again." We convinced our players that losses and personal setbacks were often opportunities in disguise. A positive approach to negative circumstances served us well.

Looking back on some of the adverse experiences our team

went through, I often see the importance of faith. We had faith that if we continued to persevere, we would eventually experience success. The type of success I was certain we would experience would not necessarily translate into wins and losses, but would stem from being faithful to what God called us to do.

9

Teamwork

> *Now this is the law of the jungle—*
> *As old and as true as the sky;*
> *And the wolf that keep it may prosper,*
> *But the wolf that shall break it must die.*
> *As the creeper that girdles the tree trunk,*
> *The law runneth forward and back—*
> *And the strength of the pack is the wolf*
> *And the strength of the wolf is the pack.*
> **—Rudyard Kipling**

We live in a culture that is strongly oriented toward the individual. The title of the best-selling book *Looking Out for Number One,* by Robert Ringer, exemplifies the prevalent, self-absorbed perspective of our culture. This me-first attitude often permeates athletic teams as well.

The essence of teamwork is servanthood. When players see the needs of others being as important as their own needs, they begin to reach out to those around them. They attempt to make others better and are primarily concerned with team success. As one player reaches out to another and demonstrates a willingness to sacrifice personal goals for team objectives, the attitude often spreads. The prevailing attitude on a team can be that of self-sacrifice and concern for the team. The reverse is also true in that selfishness and self-interest breed increased dissension and alienation among team members.

As I examined my faith, I realized that Jesus was a man for others. What He did was sacrifice Himself, and in so doing, He not only honored God but drew others to Him. In John 13:15–16, after washing his disciples' feet, Jesus says, "I have set you an example that you should do as I have done for you. I tell you the truth, no servant is greater than his master nor is a messenger greater than the one who sent him."

As a coach, there is a temptation to consider oneself preeminent and look at players as pieces of the puzzle who enable the coach to achieve his goals. When I viewed myself as a servant of the other coaches and the players, things went better on our team and for me personally. This did not mean that I was any less demanding or did not expect great effort and solid preparation. It did mean, however, that I was there to do whatever I could to help them accomplish team objectives and mature into better people.

Most Nebraska football players were the best players on their respective high school teams. Some were considered the best ever to play at their high schools and were often seen as indispensable to the success of their team. An environment that places the student-athlete in the spotlight can lead to self-centeredness and a preoccupation with personal objectives.

Players seemed to operate out of two primary stances. The "what is in it for me?" attitude generally caused an athlete to be concerned with his own well-being, the amount of recognition he received, and what the team or organization was going to do to ensure his personal success. A player displaying the "what can I contribute?" attitude, however, placed more emphasis on what he could do for his teammates rather than the individual attention and praise he might receive. Very few players are either totally self-centered or totally altruistic; generally they possess elements of both selfishness and self-sacrifice within their personalities. However, during their competitive careers, athletes fall into one category or the other most of the time. Professional basketball player Magic Johnson recognized the importance of the spirit of self-sacrifice and contribution as he paraphrased President Kennedy in saying, "Ask not what your teammates can do for you. Ask what you can do for your teammates."

One of the most difficult challenges of coaching, particularly in recent years, has been shifting the attitude of as many players as possible from self-interest to being team-oriented. Much of the success we experienced at Nebraska was due, in part, to many players placing team goals and team welfare ahead of personal desires. Knute Rockne, legendary football coach at Notre Dame, once said, "The secret of winning football games is working more as a team, less as individuals. I play not my eleven best but my best eleven."

Successful seasons often instill a deeper sense of pride and commitment within the individuals connected to a program. As we had success on the football field and as several team records were set, I often heard players comment that they did not want to be part of a team that failed to maintain those records and performance standards. Through the 1998 season, Nebraska had 37 consecutive winning seasons, winning at least nine games for 30 straight years. The players felt a responsibility not only to the program but to the men who had preceded them as well. Our players and coaches cared about the program to an unusual degree and were willing to pay a great price to ensure a continuation of excellence. Once a football program or organization reaches a point where the people involved begin to feel that type of loyalty, great things begin to happen.

During fall camp in 1989, I was in the football offices one night at 10:30 P.M. We had had an early practice that morning, an afternoon meeting and practice, and then an evening meeting. Following such a long day, I thought everyone was exhausted and had left by that hour. However, I heard some voices echoing down the hallway and went to investigate. I saw Rich Bell, our senior wingback, in a meeting room with all of the freshmen receivers. Rich was at the blackboard drawing pass plays and blocking assignments, helping a group of freshmen learn their assignments. Rich had to be tired from the day's activities and could have been in his room resting but elected to spend time helping his new teammates adjust to the system. The fact that these freshmen were fellow receivers, and would be competing for his position, indicated the extent of Rich's commitment to the team.

Rich was an outgoing wingback from Los Angeles with a ready smile and willingness to reach out to other people. He cared a great deal about Nebraska having a good team and was willing to make personal sacrifices to see that it would happen.

Rich was representative of many players on our team who made an extra effort to incorporate freshman athletes into the team. They did away with hazing new players, quite common on most teams, and went out of their way to show concern. They tried to help the freshmen adjust to life away from home and all of the pressures of major college football.

The prevailing emotion on many teams is fear. Fear of failure, the coaches, and what others might think can become pervasive among the players. The traditional coaching style is often that of a drill sergeant who motivates through intimidation and fear. This leadership style is not limited to football coaching, as many other organizations employ similar leadership styles.

As the years went by, I became more convinced that love was stronger than any other source of motivation, even fear. Vince Lombardi explained, "Teamwork is what the Green Bay Packers were all about. They didn't do it for individual glory, they did it because they loved one another." Players can work together without caring about each other, but the chemistry and synergy among a team is much greater when the people engaged in a common endeavor are bonded together by love and a shared mission.

Two elements are necessary for effective teamwork. First, the individuals who constitute the team must share a common objective, one that is important enough to them that they are willing to make sacrifices in order to achieve it. Second, team members need to care about each other in a way that eventually leads to selflessness and a common concern for others on the team.

In the spring of 1998, I attended an event in Jackson, Wyoming. I sat next to the Commandant of the United States Marines, General Charles C. Krulak. After he learned that I had been a coach, our topic of conversation turned to young people and the changes in our culture that affected them. General Krulak told me that there had been changes in the Marine Corps training procedures because traditional methods were no longer producing desired results. Historically, basic training stripped trainees of all dignity. Heads were often shaved and all traces of individuality were eliminated. Basic training was a time of sleep deprivation, physical and mental exhaustion, and treatment from superiors that left the recruit feeling less than human. This type of training was thought to promote submission to authority and a willingness to obey orders irrespective of danger.

According to the Marine Corp Commandant, the old way of

doing things has been found wanting. The military still expects discipline and obedience, but it has found more effective ways of instilling these traits. General Krulak said that studies of military organizations suggested bravery in combat did not result from a blind obedience to orders but rather from a desire to not let others down. If a military unit is bonded by love and mutual concern, soldiers are more apt to perform courageously in the face of danger to help their comrades.

Football coaching methods have often resembled the "basic training" mentality of the military. Coaches have subjected players to extreme and often inhumane treatment. Many coaches have taken away a player's individuality and sense of self-worth through humiliation and intimidation in an effort to develop players who will follow instruction without question. While the "boot camp" mentality often resulted in compliant athletes, it did not create a sense of mutual respect and caring among the team members.

At Nebraska, our coaching staff was encouraged to genuinely love and care about their players. In other words, each of them was expected to demonstrate an unconditional positive regard toward the player's total well-being. Love, in this case, does not refer to a warm, fuzzy feeling but rather to doing what is in the best interest, long term, of the young men on the team.

Players were subjected to discipline and held to high expectations. Since we believed in the importance of getting a college education, a player who did not attend class was not allowed to compete on the field. We also felt that steroid use, despite enhancing performance, was detrimental to the players' health. Therefore, we tested regularly for steroids and other drugs.

Not everyone could be a first-team player. Those who exhibited great effort deserved to play ahead of those players who chose not to put forth a consistent effort. As a result, changes on the depth chart were not uncommon. Many times an athlete's sense of self-worth is so wrapped up in his or her playing status that a drop on the depth chart can be devastating. When a player was demoted, we tried to help him see that the move was based on performance and did not mean that we had less personal regard for him.

Discipline aimed at creating the best outcome for the individual player, as well as the entire team, was important. The players knew that concern for their well-being was at the heart of discipline. We wanted each player to understand that we were concerned about him, not only as an athlete but as a person. It was not uncommon to hear a coach talk to a player about his concerns, his family, or even his social life. If a player had been dropped by his girlfriend, if things were not going well with his family at home, or if a friend or relative had died, we tried to be sensitive to that issue and spend extra time with him. There were times that I had to inform a player of the death of a parent, brother, or sister. These were difficult tasks; sometimes there was not much that could be said, and all one could do was to be present for the young man in his grief.

There were certainly times, however, when the pressure to win, or not knowing about a player's problem, interfered with our being sensitive to every player's needs. I recall an instance where a player who had exceptional talent suddenly began to perform at a subpar level.

We were in the middle of the season, and I was consumed by all of the details involved in running a football team. I was discouraged by the change in the player's performance but didn't take the time to have an extensive visit with him. Several weeks after his performance started to deteriorate, I found out that his parents had separated and were going through a divorce. From all appearances, the player had come from an ideal family; everyone, including the player, was shocked by the divorce. His performance on the field reflected the chaos his personal life was in. Had I taken the time to ask a few questions and better understand the player, we might have eased some of the player's distress and helped his on-field performance as well.

It was understood, however, that the general atmosphere on the team was supportive and caring. Players realized that they would not be asked to do something that was not in their best interest. It did not matter whether a player was a fourth-team walk-on or a first-team All-American candidate—when players were confident that their personal welfare was taken seriously, they would often become more concerned about the well-being of their fellow players and coaches.

As a coaching staff, we felt it was important to foster awareness of what was going on with each player. We gained a better sense of each player's state of mind through structured individual conferences. The assistant coaches met with the players they coached at least twice a year, once at the end of the football season and again following spring football practice. The coaches visited with each player about his performance and what he needed to do to improve not only his skills but also his contribution to the team. The coaches were also encouraged to discuss how each young man was feeling about things, both on and off the field. Toward the end of spring football, I met with each player on the team individually. Although it took a great deal of time to meet personally with all 150 players, I got to know each player better and wanted him to know that I was accessible. Often players discussed feelings, hopes, and aspirations that I would not have otherwise been aware of.

The player meetings sometimes revealed a wide discrepancy between the player's perception of his ability and his coaches' perception, which usually raised a red flag. Often a player considered himself to be a first-team player, when in reality he had third-team ability. Such discrepancies in perceived abilities were difficult to resolve. The player usually left the team, often transferring to another school where he thought he would get to play more. More often than not, the player would find that his new set of coaches evaluated his abilities to be much the same as the Nebraska coaches had perceived them to be. It seemed that transferring seldom led to improved circumstances.

The formal meeting in the spring was helpful; however, the most effective communication I had with the players often occurred in the weight room. Players were required to do 15 to 20 minutes of lifting after practice, and I would usually drop by the weight room to do some lifting myself. Working out together (I must admit that I was lifting much less strenuously than the players) created a more informal environment that allowed me to converse with a dozen or so players each evening. Throughout a season, I was able to interact several times with almost every player on the squad. Usually, the conversation was fairly light and casual, but if I sensed a player was struggling with something, I would take him aside for a more serious talk. Informal discussions in the weight room, the training room, or the dining hall were spontaneous and motivated by a genuine interest in the players. It is difficult to know your players if you don't spend time with them, and we tried to make sure that we took the time.

Fighting was not tolerated during practice. Sometimes emotions would run high and there would be some pushing and shoving. Occasionally, one player would take a swing at another player. When this happened, the players involved were required to run stadium steps. Fortunately, Memorial Stadium was high enough that running the steps got a player's attention very quickly. As a result, we held fighting to a minimum. The only time this method of discipline backfired short term was when I sent one of our tackles to the top of the stadium for fighting. By the time he reached the top, he was so fatigued that it took him 30 minutes to recover enough to make it back down. His legs had turned to jelly and he ended up missing nearly half of the practice. But his trip to the top of the stadium convinced him that fisticuffs didn't pay off. From that point on, he was much less combative.

Our coaching staff took a strong stance against fighting because we felt that such activity often engendered negative feelings that were carried off the field and fostered resentment within the team. Furthermore, we thought individuals who could not control their emotions on the practice field would likely not contain their emotions in a football game, perhaps costing the team a personal foul or a player ejection at a critical time.

A great example of the importance of controlling emotion occurred in the 1995 Orange Bowl versus Miami. Feelings ran high, and the Miami players were very vocal because they led 10–7 at halftime. We emphasized discipline and self-control during the intermission. I told our players that if they would not retaliate or talk back, Miami would get flagged at a key point and the penalty would contribute to our winning the game. I was proud of our players' composure throughout the game and particularly in the second half. Miami was hurt badly by a personal foul penalty at a critical time. Often when one player punches another, the player hit retaliates, and there are offsetting penalties. Our players did not retaliate, however, and we went on to win the game and the national championship.

At Nebraska, it was evident that our players cared not only about the program but also for each other. This mutual compassion resulted in a higher level of achievement, which, in turn, contributed to more players caring about the team and each other. Success and caring complemented each other as key components of our football program. Caring, however, preceded success.

Not long after the Unity Council was formed, we began to show a five-minute "psych-up" tape just before boarding the buses to depart for the stadium on game day. These tapes usually began by showing about a dozen key plays we had made in the previous week's game. The big plays left the players with positive images of the team's talent and effectiveness.

The most effective part of the tapes, however, were spontaneous clips of players expressing their feelings about teammates, coaches, and the football program. The more the players knew how much their teammates cared about them, the stronger their common bond became. A team inspired by love is a team without fear. The Bible says that "perfect love casts out fear." Fear gets in the way of effective performance; love enables us to perform without hesitation or self-doubt. It is very freeing to feel valued and cared for by your coaches and teammates irrespective of success or failure on the field.

We have had many great teams at Nebraska, but the 1994 team possessed the strongest shared vision of any team that I've been associated with. The near miss on the national championship the year before against Florida State and the desire to return to the national championship game and win it resulted in unusual resolve among the team. Each player expressed confidence that the team could play at the national-championship level in 1994. Of the teams I have been associated with, the 1994 team had the strongest love, unity, and chemistry. These qualities enabled them to achieve far beyond the sum of their abilities.

Our 1994 game with Colorado exemplified what teamwork can do. That year Colorado had the most talented team I recalled their ever having. They had 16 returning starters from their excellent 1993 team. Their quarterback, Kordell Stewart, was an outstanding athlete who later had an outstanding career in the NFL. Rashaan Salaam played running back and was so talented that he won the Heisman Trophy. They had great receivers such as Michael Westbrook and several defensive players who later went on to have outstanding professional careers. Our starting quarterback, Tommie Frazier, was out with a serious injury. We were talented even without Tommie, but we were considerably shy of the personnel level of Colorado. Our defense played a tremendous game. We were so unified and consistent that a great Colorado offense was limited to only one touchdown. Our offense played equally well. Brook Berringer stepped up at quarterback and played a nearly flawless game. Our teamwork and precision was such that we moved the ball consistently and beat Colorado soundly by a score of 24–7.

That same season, we defeated a very good Kansas State team in Manhattan, Kansas, on a cold, rainy day. Tommie Frazier was still out with an injury and Brook Berringer had suffered a collapsed lung in each of the two preceding games, but our defense played so well that we kept Kansas State out of the end zone, and we won 19–6 in a great team effort. Baron Miles covered Kansas State's best receiver and knocked away passes on several occasions in one of the finest cornerback performances I have seen.

The 1997 team was similar to the 1994 team. We had experienced two disappointing losses in the 1996 season and displayed tremendous drive in 1997 to win the national championship. This focus eliminated outside distractions. In addition, this group of young men generated great team chemistry as they compiled a 13–0 record.

The 1994 and 1997 teams stand out in my memory as teams that demonstrated exceptional teamwork, which eventually resulted in national championships. Both teams were talented, yet their ability was not any better than that of many other teams. The defining characteristic of these teams was their commitment to teamwork. They knew how to pull together and play for a shared vision, which united them as a whole unit.

The "talk" that comes from a team is often indicative of team attitude. A few years ago, a professional coach described his team as "not very good." He went on to say that he did not think his team would win many more games because they just weren't playing well. His statements proved to be prophetic, as what had been thought to be a very good team lost nearly all of its remaining games. More often than not, players will play up or down to the level of confidence the coach displays in them. I believed it was very important that the comments our coaches made about our football team reflected a confident attitude toward our chances of winning. If players sense their coaches don't have faith in them, they will often turn the coaches' concerns into a reality. Faith in one's coaches and teammates is critical to confident performance.

When a big game approaches, I often hear coaches make a very dangerous comment. They say that their team must play a "perfect game" in order to win. Such a statement indicates to the players that their normal level of play will not be good enough; that the talent of the upcoming opponent leaves no margin for error. This interpretation frequently causes a team to try too hard. They are "tight" and unable to perform at the level of which they are capable. With time, our coaching staff came to realize that approaching "big" games and "little" games in much the same manner led to consistency, confidence, and teamwork.

The "talk" among the players is even more important than what the coaches say publicly about the team. Like most people, football players have a tendency to complain about their problems among each other. They often express displeasure over the lack of playing time, demands of coaches, equipment, medical care, and even academic supervision.

We talked to our players repeatedly about the importance of addressing issues that were bothering them with people who could do something about resolving the problem. Rather than complaining to other players, friends, or family, we encouraged them to discuss the problem with the person directly involved.

If there was a problem between a player and a coach, the player needed to approach the coach rather than discuss the conflict with other players. Any problems regarding uniforms and equipment were to be directed to the equipment manager, because he had control over such items. If a player did not feel that we were running or throwing the ball enough, or disagreed with the defensive scheme, he was encouraged to visit with the head coach or the appropriate offensive or defensive coordinator. In any organization, approaching the individuals directly involved with the problem often results in finding satisfactory solutions. Grousing and complaining only created a negative atmosphere. The Unity Council provided an effective forum for clearing the air. If players had problems with a member of the coaching staff or support staff, that person would attend a Unity

Council meeting and differences would be ironed out. Often, the staff member was not aware of a problem until being contacted by the Unity Council.

Comments by captains and other team leaders were particularly crucial to team morale. Leadership sets the tone for any organization. If leaders are positive and proactive, positive behavior usually follows. When leaders are negative, their organizations usually perform in a negative manner.

We found that positive statements in the locker room, the training room, and in the weight room increased our success as a team. Most players recognized the destructiveness of negative comments, and the "team talk" was generally positive.

The emphasis placed on direct confrontation and positive attitudes paid off. Players often approached individuals who seemed disgruntled and resolved the problem themselves rather than have personal animosities spread throughout the team. Many times the players resolved issues that coaches were not even aware of. If two players were not getting along, we pulled them aside and discussed their differences. Most disputes were quickly resolved and nothing festered and lingered on.

When players of the same position encouraged and pulled for each other, team chemistry was greatly enhanced. On the other hand, when a player standing on the sideline hoped that his competition would fumble the ball or miss a tackle, team unity was just as easily destroyed. Wishing bad things on an opponent or teammate does not help anyone perform at his best.

I met with the quarterbacks daily, and since quarterback disputes can easily divide a team, I was especially sensitive to friction among them. On one occasion, our second quarterback complained that the starting quarterback was not allowing him his share of passes during the pregame warm-up period. I met with both players and discussed the matter further. The number-one quarterback thought it was more important that he get loosened up and complained that his backup often got in the way. We developed a system of rotation that was satisfactory, and the two players, even though they were never close, developed a decent working relationship. For the most part, however, our quarterbacks got along well and were good friends on and off the field. They spent a great deal of time together in meetings, and their common quarterbacking challenges drew them into good friendships.

During the season, I encouraged the players and coaches not to read the sports pages or listen to radio talk shows. Even when a team is performing well and winning, many negative opinions are expressed. Often those who are critical have a very limited knowledge of that which they are criticizing. The best way to get through the season was to focus on the task at hand and to be as positive as possible—reading and hearing negative comments was not helpful.

In visiting with one of our quarterbacks, I noticed he seemed to be down. When I inquired about his problem, he indicated that several negative letters had been sent to his apartment. The letters really hurt the young quarterback, to the point where his confidence was shaken. Most were unsigned, and I advised him to throw away anything unsigned without reading it.

My secretary, Mary Lyn, was very good at sorting out the unsigned letters addressed to me. She knew that my reading correspondence the author would not even sign would not lead to anything productive.

Negativism in our culture has become so pervasive that it seems to pull everyone down. Many years ago, one of my assistant coaches was very analytical about our offense. He took up a great deal of meeting time reviewing why something would not work. When asked what would work, he often had little to offer. Our staff was more interested in hearing about what would work than what would not. Without a positive, proactive approach, little gets done.

As a head coach, I believed it was as important to want the best for the coaching staff as well as for the players. When an assistant coach considers taking a job elsewhere, it can be tempting to discourage him from leaving, or to not give him a whole-hearted job recommendation when people call about him. My philosophy, however, was to do what was in the best interests of the coach. This included letting him make his own decision as to whether he should leave our program, as well as providing prospective employers with the best possible recommendation when they inquired. My actions were not motivated by a desire to get rid of the coach. In fact, in almost every case, I wanted him to stay. However, I also wanted him to feel that there were no strings attached to our relationship and that I wanted what was best for him. These men needed to choose the best possible situation for themselves and their families. Therefore, I felt that the coaches who stayed at Nebraska really wanted to be there and never felt as though they had been trapped or coerced into staying.

I recall one of our assistant coaches being offered a head coaching position at his undergraduate institution. I assumed that he would take the job, but the more he thought about it, the more he was convinced that what he really wanted was to stay at Nebraska. Had I pressured him to stay, I'm sure that I would have driven him away. As it was, he worked through his decision at his own pace, was happy with his decision to stay, and continued to be very productive for us as a team.

A positive team attitude elevates a team to the point where the whole is greater than the sum of its parts. Teams can transcend their talent level with exceptional chemistry but also fall far short of their potential when there is division and strife within the team. We found that an emphasis on team contribution rather than personal goals, an environment that was caring and supportive, positive talk within the team, and good communication were keys to exceptional team chemistry.

■ 10 ■

Moving On

To get men to do what they don't want to do in order to achieve what they want to achieve. That's what coaching is all about. That's the challenge I will miss.
—**Tom Landry, former Dallas Cowboys coach**

As I participated in athletics through high school, college, and professional football, I did not plan to be a coach. For some reason, coaching did not appeal to me, and I assumed that I would end up either in business or in college administration work.

My career in the National Football League was never particularly illustrious, but I did feel that I was capable of playing for a number of years. During the 1961 season, I severely injured my hamstring. Despite the injury, I played every game with the aid of a weekly shot of novocaine. While playing through the injury, however, I developed scar tissue in the hamstring and did not recover in the off-season. As I tried to work out in preparation for the 1962 season, the hamstring kept knotting up and I realized that I was through as a player.

My inability to return to football made me decide to attend graduate school at the University of Nebraska in the spring semester of 1962. I began to suffer withdrawal pains; athletics had been the major focus of my life since I had been nine or ten years old. At age 25, it was difficult to give it up. Therefore, I approached Bob Devaney about a graduate assistant coaching position. Following a successful career at the University of Wyoming, Bob had just been hired as the head football coach at the University of Nebraska. Sensing my desire to stay involved in athletics, Bob gave me a position that fell somewhere between a graduate assistant and an unpaid volunteer coach.

At the time, Bob was having trouble with a group of players living in Selleck Quadrangle, one of the men's dormitories. Ten players lived in one wing of the dorm. Most were from Chicago and were not adapting well to Lincoln, Nebraska. Successfully intimidating the student dorm counselors, the players ran their dormitory wing as they saw fit—and often this did not include much academic endeavor. Bob felt it would be a good idea if I roomed with one of the problem players in order to keep an eye on them. In exchange, I received free room and board.

There were times when I felt undercompensated. There were occasional fights and unruly behavior. However, I eventually developed a good relationship with the players and things became more quiet and orderly in that part of Selleck Quadrangle. I still occasionally hear from some of those athletes. It has been surprising to see how many of them have become quite successful. Three have done very well in business, one is an attorney, one is a successful football coach, one is a judge, one is an English teacher, and another runs a large funeral home. I learned early on that "problem" players often become constructive citizens.

During spring football, I also did some coaching and found that I liked it. The experience was a nice diversion from my graduate studies. I also met a young lady named Nancy that spring. She had already signed a contract to teach in California following her graduation. I was sure that we were right for each other. I convinced her that long-distance romances were not a good idea, and we married later in the summer. Nancy knew about my living conditions in the dormitory and thought it would be a good idea to live in an apartment, so I said good-bye to the Chicago group and began to seriously consider what I wanted to do professionally.

Graduate work became serious business. I wanted to complete my degree as quickly as possible. I continued to coach and received my master's degree in June of 1963. At this time, I was also asked to do some teaching in the educational psychology department. I'm not certain how I survived the next two years or how Nancy put up with me. I was teaching four classes, taking a full graduate load, writing a doctoral dissertation, and also spending many hours each week with the football program. I finished my Ph.D. in August of 1965 and was confused as to what I wanted to do. My graduate work was directed toward a life in academics, yet

I was drawn more and more toward coaching. I could not decide which path to take. Therefore, I bought more time by increasing my coaching duties while still teaching classes in the educational psychology department.

I received pressure from both Bob Devaney and the educational psychology faculty to commit myself to either coaching or teaching. Eventually, I realized I was not prepared to leave athletics. After two years of sitting on the fence, I told Bob I wanted to be a full-time coach. I was 28 years old and felt that time was slipping away. Therefore, I decided I would give coaching everything I had for the next seven years. If I was not a head coach by age 35, I thought I would be past my prime as a coach and would pursue the academic career track. Looking back on that period from the perspective of a "retired" coach, my impatience is hard to understand. I was driven to accomplish something, yet I was not sure where this ambition would lead.

I did not want to follow Bob Devaney at Nebraska. With his engaging personality and high level of success, anyone who followed Bob would struggle to survive. I interviewed for the head football coaching position at the University of South Dakota and the selection process came down to one other finalist and myself. The search committee decided to hire the other person. A year later, I was offered the head football coaching job at Augustana College in Sioux Falls, South Dakota. Nancy and I thought seriously about this opportunity and were on the verge of accepting the position. At the same time, however, Bob Devaney decided that he wanted me to stay at Nebraska. He had George Cook, the president of a Lincoln insurance firm, take me to lunch. George was persuasive; he talked me out of the Augustana job and convinced me to stay with Division I football.

In December of 1969, I was one of two finalists being considered for the head coaching position at Texas Tech. At age 32, I found this job very appealing. Tech had a good program and West Texas was a lot like Nebraska. Recently, in January of 1999, I received a letter from Grover Murray, who was the president of Texas Tech when I interviewed there 30 years ago. Grover indicated that I had been his first choice, but that others favored another finalist, who had head coaching experience. The people at Texas Tech chose the other finalist. It was a major letdown.

That same year, Bob Devaney indicated that he was about to step aside and wanted me to be the head coach. By this time, I realized how difficult it was to get a head coaching job at a major university. So, despite my misgivings about following Bob, I told him that I would stay at Nebraska and take over when he was done coaching. Two years later, Bob publicly announced that the 1972 season would be his last as head coach and that I would be the next head coach at Nebraska.

Following that somewhat circuitous path into the coaching profession, I eventually spent 36 years coaching, all at the University of Nebraska. I was a graduate assistant and assistant under Bob for eleven years. My last 25 years of coaching were as a head coach. Coaching was certainly very time consuming and intense. However, I loved the strategy involved in the game, and I enjoyed interacting with the athletes and coaches very much.

Money has never been a high priority. If coaching had been only a way to make a living, it would not have held my interest for so many years. I saw coaching as more of a mission. It provided me with an opportunity to make a difference in the lives of young people. This perspective gave coaching an added dimension of meaning and significance.

Letting go of something that has required such a commitment of time and energy is never easy. In coaching, the lows are lower and the highs are higher than in any occupation I can think of. I will miss the feeling of elation, unity, and love that accompanies a significant win. It wasn't the win itself, or the trophy, or the ring, it was the powerful emotional bond that was formed. The feeling in the locker room after beating Miami for the national championship following the 1994 season, the tremendous commitment of the 1995 team, and the love expressed after the final game of the 1997 season are feelings I will likely never experience again. Vince Lombardi reflected on his departure from coaching by saying, "What I missed most was—well, it wasn't the tension and the crowds and game on Sunday. And it certainly wasn't the winning. And it wasn't the spotlight and all that. . . . There's a great . . . closeness on a football team, you know—a rapport between the men and the coach that's like no other sport. It's a binding together, a knitting together. For me, it's like father and sons, and that's what I missed. I missed the players coming to me."

Leaving a job properly is important. If handled the right way, the organization suffers minimal disruption and those who take over have a good chance of being successful. Leaving at the right time, for the right reasons, and with the right people taking over is often a difficult task to accomplish, particularly in athletics.

Several football coaching changes occurred at the conclusion of the 1998 season. In several instances, head coaches or key assistants accepted new assignments and left their teams without coaching their team's postseason bowl games. In the past, it has been customary for a coach to finish out the season; however, it now seems that coaches move to greener pastures even before their duties for the season are complete. Others leave abruptly during the middle of recruiting season. This pattern of change is often disruptive and disillusioning to the players on those teams.

A great deal of thought and consideration went into my decision to step aside at Nebraska. Many factors made it likely that the 1997 season would be my last. First, I had made promises to two key people that I wouldn't coach beyond a certain point in time. My time was up. The only unknown variable was whether or not someone from within the staff would be promoted to the head coaching position. As I mentioned earlier in this book, if my leaving had resulted in a coach from another school taking over at Nebraska, I would not have stepped aside. Such a decision would have left my assistant coaches and their families without any assurance of having jobs. There was no way I could leave under such circumstances. Fortunately, I was given assurances that my coaching staff would remain intact and continue at Nebraska. Therefore, I was determined to stick with my commitment, and I realized that my coaching days at Nebraska were about over.

Second, my coaching style was such that I was not sure how much longer I could maintain the pace. I coached the quarterbacks and performed most of the duties of an offensive coordinator during the last years of Bob Devaney's coaching tenure and continued in that capacity throughout my 25 years as head coach. Most coaches appoint offensive and defensive coordinators to manage those areas. The head coach is then free to deal with things like the press, booster groups, and administrative details. In such situations, however, the head coach is often relatively uninvolved in strategy, play calling, and game management.

I did not want to coach that way. For me, the enjoyment of coaching was to coordinate the offense, call the plays, and keep tabs on what the defense was doing. I wanted to be immersed in the game itself. This approach took a lot of time and required much attention to detail. I had to spend at least 30 hours a week analyzing game tapes of our upcoming opponent to do an effective job of calling plays. In addition, there were staff meetings, player meetings, practices, press conferences, and correspondence to attend to. Working 80- to 90-hour weeks seven days a week for seven straight months was getting so grueling that I wasn't sure I could continue. However, I didn't want to coach if I wasn't going to be hands-on. The most enjoyable part of coaching was the day-to-day strategy and working directly with the players and the coaches.

Once the game started, I wanted to be an active participant. I wanted to be involved in game adjustments if our opponents came up with something unexpected. Head coaches who act primarily as administrators, delegating nearly all of the coaching responsibility to assistants, are often at the mercy of their offensive and defensive coordinator's competence level once the game starts. They are so far removed from the nuts and bolts of football that they cannot effectively contribute to the decision making during an actual game.

Third, my interest in coaching was still at a peak. We had been one of the top NCAA Division I football teams for several years, and the game still intrigued me. This fascination with football was another factor I considered before stepping aside. I felt it was important to leave while I was still involved and interested in the game. There wasn't a whole lot more that we could accomplish as a team that we hadn't already done. I was concerned that my interest and intensity level had reached a point where I might not be able to sustain it.

Fourth, as the years passed, I realized that Nancy and our children had paid a greater price than I had realized as I pursued my coaching career. It was not fair to coach until I was so decrepit that I had nothing left to give my family.

The final factor in my decision to leave was my bout, discussed earlier in this book, with an irregular heartbeat. Even though this was not a life-threatening condition, I took it as a final sign indicating that my coaching days were over.

The commitments I had made, the willingness of the university administration to name Frank Solich as my successor, family considerations, and health matters all combined to signal the end of my coaching career at Nebraska. I knew that I would miss coaching, but I hoped there was something ahead of me that would still give life meaning and excitement. Poet Robert Frost once described my perspective at the time: "In three words I can sum up everything I have learned about life: It goes on."

Coaching is hard to leave, especially when things are going well. One difficulty with leaving coaching is that it is not a profession from which one can phase out. In many professions, an individual can gradually cut back on the required workload. A doctor treats fewer patients, an attorney works fewer hours, and a barber takes an extra day off. Coaching, however, does not work that way. There is no middle ground; either you are a coach or you are not. It is virtually impossible to hold a coaching job while easing out of the profession. Doing so is unfair to the players and coaches who are counting on you.

Fortunately, I had the "luxury" of one final recruiting season. Following the 1997 season, I told Frank Solich that I would be willing to stay involved through the recruiting process. By doing so, I could help ease the transition for our players and also reassure the young men we were recruiting that there would be little change at Nebraska. Even though I would no longer be there, the coaching staff would remain intact and the philosophy and culture of the organization would be much the same.

During the months of December and January, I saw all of the recruits who visited Nebraska and I stayed active until the national signing date in early February. However, after the bowl game with Tennessee on January 2, 1998, things changed. Frank was now the head coach, and I was a lame duck trying to finish things out the best I could.

I'm sure this situation was a little awkward for Frank. Sometimes the coaches would turn to me for a decision during recruiting meetings. This occurred out of habit, and sometimes, again out of habit, I would respond. In such instances, I needed to bite my tongue, back off, and make sure that Frank was in charge. I was able to assist in recruiting a solid group of players and helped ease the transition process. However, it became very clear that the time had come to stay away and let Frank be the coach. My final act of leaving was to do just that—to clear out of the athletic department and find an office elsewhere. After making the final move, I still occasionally showed up in the athletic department. Only now, I was not part of the coaching staff. I acted more as a support person. Although I was physically removed, I wanted the players and coaches to know that I still cared.

My predecessor, Bob Devaney, exemplified how best to leave coaching. Even though Bob was a tremendously successful coach and probably had qualms about how a 35-year-old would perform, he never interfered. As athletic director, he could have given all kinds of advice, publicly or privately, that would have been disruptive. Instead, Bob was always supportive, loyal, and never intrusive.

Upon the announcement in December of 1997 that I was going to quit coaching, the media frequently referred to my "retirement." I don't recall ever using the term myself, as I don't believe in retirement. I referred to "stepping aside," as I felt that I was going to remain very active even though I would no longer be a football coach. The word "retirement" was used in conjunction with my leaving football so often that most people assumed I was committed to a life of leisure.

Often, I was approached by fans asking me how I was enjoying "retirement." Since I was sure that I would miss coaching, I deliberately overscheduled myself to avoid staring at the walls and feeling sorry for myself. The irony of such inquiries was that I was now as busy as ever—or busier. After one or two attempts to explain what I was doing to inquiring fans, I realized that there was no way I could adequately explain how I felt or describe what I was doing. I simply began to answer their questions about "retirement" by saying that everything was "fine."

I was apprehensive about "retirement." I recall Alabama's Bear Bryant saying that he would probably "croak" if he ever quit coaching. He did just that—he died only a few months after he ended his career. Health problems are not unusual when one's central purpose in life has been removed.

My hobby is fishing, particularly fly-fishing. However, I enjoy all kinds of fishing—trolling, spin casting, or even just watching a bobber suspended above a worm or a minnow. Upon "retirement," it was tempting to just go fishing in Alaska, Canada, South Dakota, and Montana in the summer and the Florida Keys and Central America in the winter. Sometimes, during a long football season, I thought about fishing. Just a half-day of fishing would have restored my soul. Now I had a chance to fish and relax all that I wanted. Intuitively, however, I knew that fishing day after day would eventually grow old. It would be enjoyable for a while but devoid of meaning.

A meaningless existence can be fatal. I knew that someone with a high energy level who has been involved in an occupation as intense as coaching often doesn't last very long if he or she abruptly quits and does little or nothing. When one no longer has a purpose in life, life itself often shuts down. Bobby Bowden once said, "After retirement, there ain't but one or two big events left." Retirement is often a psychological death for those who have found meaning only in their work.

I had offers to serve as a radio commentator on Nebraska football broadcasts. It seemed, however, that there was no way I could do this without being perceived as a "Monday morning quarterback." Since it was important to support Frank Solich and his coaching staff, I declined these offers.

I assessed my situation. My energy level was excellent, my health was reasonably good, and, at age 60, I still had some good years left. I found I was still passionate about one thing, and that was young people. Seeing young people grow and develop always renews and excites me. Continuing to work with young people would afford me the opportunity to do something that was meaningful and energizing.

Still having academic rank at the university, although I had not been in the classroom in 30 years, I decided that returning to my academic roots might be something I would enjoy. Since coaches often have a great impact on young people, I felt that teaching a football coaching class would be both interesting and rewarding. In academic circles, such a class is not highly regarded. However, as our culture has unraveled and as families have disintegrated, coaches have been expected to assume additional responsibility for the well-being of the young people with whom they work. Coaching, at its best, has truly become a calling.

Values affecting family stability have been challenged. In order to maintain a desired standard of living, often both parents work, leaving much child care in the hands of others. The divorce rate has skyrocketed and the welfare of children has become less important to our culture.

A coach often fills the void that exists in the lives of troubled and neglected young people. Athletes often reflect the values and attitudes of those who coach them. For many of them, the coach is the only stable, constant adult in their lives. By teaching aspiring coaches, I believe that I can indirectly impact many young people. If I can convince just a few young coaches that caring about and nurturing their athletes is not going to adversely affect the win-loss record, the effort will be worthwhile.

In addition to the football coaching class, I was also asked to teach a graduate class in athletic administration. Even though I was far from an expert in the field, I welcomed that challenge, as well. Athletic administration has evolved into a complex combination of people skills and business acumen.

Although teaching has been a very important part of my transition out of coaching, mentoring has been my main interest. In 1991, my wife Nancy and I began a mentoring program in Lincoln. Twenty-five football players responded to an invitation to mentor junior high school boys in the Lincoln Public Schools. The players volunteered to spend time with the young person they were mentoring once a week. The young men chosen to be mentored were evaluated by counselors and teachers as being kids who would benefit from a relationship with a supportive and caring mentor. We also had monthly group meetings involving all of the mentors and mentees. On these occasions, we had a recreational activity, such as a basketball game, as well as pizza, and discussed the importance of academic achievement, goal-setting, and character issues. We wanted to expand the mentee's awareness of solid values and his potential to rise above his circumstances.

Most of these young men responded favorably to the mentoring program. We lost three of the original 25 mentees. Two moved away and one got into trouble, so we were left with 22 mentor-mentee pairs. Three years after we started the program, most of the mentees entered their freshman and sophomore years of high school. We gathered them for a meeting and presented them with a challenge. If they graduated from high school, stayed out of trouble with the law, avoided drug usage, and did not father a child out of wedlock, we would fund their college education. We asked them to sign a contract indicating their agreement to those terms. In return, we agreed to uphold our part of the bargain. I was uneasy, as I wasn't sure where the money was going to come from. Nancy and I agreed to contribute as much as we could, but realized that there would not be enough if all 22 chose to attend college. We were very fortunate, however, because a few very generous supporters donated over $200,000, a figure based on my having coached 200 wins at Nebraska. I asked that the funds be placed in the scholarship program and breathed a sigh of relief.

The results of the mentoring project have been gratifying. Of the 22 young people who stayed in the program, 20 graduated from high school and 18 went on to pursue a postsecondary education. Many of them attended a local community college, some enrolled in a trade school, and a few went to the University of Nebraska or another nearby college. Although some have not been terribly successful in their college work, we feel that having over 90 percent of the mentees graduate from high school and go on to complete at least some college work certainly beat the odds. The counselors who had originally selected those students to be mentored had indicated that the odds of their even finishing high school were not good.

I've been asked from time to time what a mentor does and why mentoring is important. The best response I can give to this question is to share a story involving my father and my grandfather. My father's name was always listed as "Charles C. Osborne." I often asked him what the middle initial C stood for. Never very fond of his middle name, my father was always evasive in response to my question. After several inquiries, I finally extracted enough information to learn that the middle initial stood for "Currins." My uncle, Howard Osborne, later explained that my father was named after an itinerant preacher named Currins who covered much of western Nebraska during my grandfather's youth.

My grandfather, Thomas Clifford Osborne, grew up on a small farm near Bayard, Nebraska. His father, my great-grandfather, was a veteran of the Civil War and reportedly was not always an ideal parent. My grandfather was the only one of four children who went to college. Currins had taken an interest in my grandfather when he was a young man. He saw potential that others, including my grandfather, himself, did not see. He provided a vision of what my grandfather might accomplish with his life. Currins encouraged my grandfather to attend college at a time when practically no one growing up on a small homestead in western Nebraska even considered college. At the turn of the century, my grandfather matriculated at Hastings College and became captain of the football team.

Being a man of strong convictions, my grandfather took an oath that he would never use alcohol. While he was working as a cowpuncher, he was bitten by a rattlesnake. At that time, the only known cure for a rattlesnake bite was a large slug of whiskey. Even though his life hung in the balance, he stuck by his oath. Fortunately for me, he survived.

Currins also encouraged my grandfather in his spiritual life. Eventually, my grandfather attended seminary and entered the ministry. He spoke several languages, including Sioux, served in the state legislature, and was very popular with the ranchers and homesteaders in western Nebraska. My grandfather was killed by lightning at age 65, when I was quite young. As I grew up, I often considered what my grandfather would want me to do. Although he was deceased, his life influenced many of my decisions.

While at Hastings College, my grandfather met a bright young woman named Julia. They later married and had five children, all of whom graduated from college during the Depression.

Currins was my grandfather's mentor. Without Currins, it is unlikely that he would have developed into the accomplished person he was. My own father's life would have been very different had Currins not mentored my grandfather. Without Currins's encouragement, my grandfather probably would have stayed on that small homestead in western Nebraska and his life, as well as the lives of his children, would not have been the same.

Mentoring has a longitudinal effect. I am certain that my life has been influenced by Currins's interest in my grandfather. The quality of my grandfather's life, and subsequently that of my father, affected me, as well. It is strange how someone whom I never met and know little about has had such a great impact on me and my family.

According to the Bible, the sins of the fathers are visited upon the children to the third and fourth generation. Abuse, alcoholism, and promiscuous behavior tend to be cyclical and self-perpetuating. An effective mentor is one who breaks the negative cycle and encourages choices that lead to a more productive life.

Currins's influence illustrates what mentoring is all about. Presently, many young people do not have an adult in their lives who believes in them. Mentoring is not advice-giving so much as it is listening, affirming, and providing a vision of what might be. A person who is valued, encouraged, and supported will usually begin to live up to positive expectations. Sometimes those who have been battered by life's circumstances receive unconditional love and acceptance for the first time in their lives from a mentor. When this happens, the person receiving mentoring can begin to experience something of what God's love is like. It is hard to conceive of God as a loving father if one has never encountered love of that type in his or her life.

If a coach tells his football team that it is no good, it is often not long before the team fulfills that prophecy by becoming worse. Just as teams can be brought down by negative expectations, so can individual athletes. If a player is told often enough by a coach or someone whom he respects that he is playing poorly, is no good, and will never be any good, his performance begins to deteriorate, and he plays so poorly that he often becomes a liability to the team. Unfortunately, many of our young people are given messages, subtly or directly, that they don't measure up and that they will never be successful at anything. "Born to lose" is one of the most common tattoos on the arms and bodies of prison inmates. These individuals have been told throughout their lifetime that they are losers and will end up in jail someday. Such statements are internalized, and the prisoners fulfill what has been said about them.

We currently have a good mentoring program in Lincoln that

involves 300 mentor-mentee matches. The young people being mentored are primarily at the seventh- and eighth-grade levels. We are attempting to add 150 mentors at the seventh-grade level each year. By the time students ranging from the seventh through the twelfth grade are being mentored, we hope to have approximately 1,000 pairs of mentors and mentees. As it grows, this mentoring effort can make a difference in Lincoln.

We have recently introduced the Teammates Program to many other communities and hope to involve nearly every Nebraska community of any size within the next five years. Teammates has provided a sense of meaning in the lives of Nancy and me, and has made the withdrawal from coaching less painful.

The future of our nation greatly concerns me. Throughout 36 years of coaching, I observed a steady deterioration in our value system and also in the amount of support provided to our young people. Many citizens seem more concerned about the economy, the government, or problems abroad. However, today's young people represent tomorrow's future. If our children continue to encounter the problems they now face, I would suggest that the major threat to our country is not the economy, the government, or foreign powers. Our greatest threat, rather, comes from within.

America will survive and be great only if we invest sufficiently in our children. Any culture depends on future generations to sustain its values and is never more than one generation removed from crumbling inward upon itself.

Ideally, the solution to the problems our young people are facing lies with intact families who have sound values. We also would benefit from a more wholesome environment. It is impossible to legislate strong family units, however. It also is very difficult to rid ourselves of negative environmental factors, such as alcohol and drug abuse, violence, promiscuity, and pornography. Mentoring appears to be one of the best available solutions to these problems at this time. Most of the difficulties facing our young people have been caused by a breakdown of important one-to-one relationships. They can best be solved by establishing new, healthy one-to-one relationships.

There is a growing awareness in our nation that things are amiss. The most pressing question facing us is whether we have the will and the commitment as a nation to provide our children with the positive role models, healthy relationships, and financial support that they so desperately need.

If we are to turn the corner and begin to reverse the flood of problems facing our nation's young people, I am convinced that a spiritual reawakening will have to be a major part of the solution. If we trust Him and honor Him, God can change the hearts and minds of His people. A major shift in our nation's spiritual consciousness would seem to be our main hope.

Although I miss coaching, and part of me will always want to experience some of those great moments again, I am excited about the future. These are difficult times. There is much hanging in the balance. It is important for all of us to engage in finding a way for our nation to survive and become an example of what a world power can be, not just financially and militarily, but also in regard to character, values, and spiritual strength.

Bibliography

Benson, Bob. *He Speaks Softly: Learning to Hear God's Voice*. Waco, TX: Word Books, 1985.

Bowden, Bobby. *More Than Just a Game*. Nashville, TN: Thomas Nelson, 1994.

Bradley, Bill. *Values of the Game*. New York: Artisan, 1998.

Bynum, Mike, ed. *Lombardi: A Dynasty Remembered*. Nashville, TN: Athlon Sports Communications, 1994.

Cooper, Kenneth H., M.D. *It's Better to Believe*. Nashville, TN: Thomas Nelson, 1995.

Covey, Stephen R. *Principle-Centered Leadership*. New York: Summit Books, 1991.

Covey, Stephen R. *The Seven Habits of Highly Effective People: Powerful Lessons in Personal Change*. New York: Simon & Schuster, 1989.

Dossey, Larry, M.D. *Healing Words: The Power of Prayer and the Practice of Medicine*. San Francisco: Harper San Francisco, 1993.

Ferguson, Howard E., and Gary Schwab. *The Edge*. Cleveland, OH: Getting The Edge Company, 1990. (Gary Schwab is listed as a "contributing author.")

Fryar, Irving. *Sunday Is My Day*. Sisters, OR: Multnomah, 1997.

Gallup, George H., Jr., and Timothy Jones. *The Saints Among Us*. Harrisburg, PA: Morehouse, 1992.

Gibbs, Joe, with Jerry Jenkins. *Joe Gibbs: Fourth and One*. Nashville, TN: Thomas Nelson, 1991.

God's Little Instruction Book: Inspirational Wisdom on How to Live a Happy and Fulfilled Life. Tulsa, OK: Honor Books, 1993.

Handley, Rod. *Character Counts—Who's Counting Yours?* Grand Island, NE: Cross Training Publishing, 1995.

Holtz, Lou. *Winning Everyday*. New York: HarperCollins, 1998.

Horn, Wade F., Ph.D. *Father Facts*, 3rd edition. Gaithersburg, MD: The National Fatherhood Initiative.

Jones, Charlie. *What Makes Winners Win: Thoughts and Reflections from Successful Athletes*. New York: Broadway Books, 1997.

Landry, Tom, with Gregg Lewis. *Tom Landry: An Autobiography*.

Grand Rapids, MI: Zondervan Publishing House; New York: HarperCollins, 1990.

Osborne, Tom, with John E. Roberts. *More Than Winning*. Nashville, TN: Thomas Nelson, 1985.

Peck, M. Scott, M.D. *People of the Lie: The Hope for Healing Human Evil*. New York: Simon and Schuster, 1985.

Quakenbush, Robert, and Mike Bynum, eds. *Knute Rockne: His Life and Legend*. N.p.: October Football Corporation, 1988. (Based on the unfinished biography of Knute Rockne.)

Riley, Pat. *The Winner Within: A Life Plan for Team Players*. New York: Berkley Books, 1993.

Rockne, Knute. *The Four Winners*. New York: Devin-Adair, 1925.

Schembechler, Bo, and Mitch Albom. *Bo*. New York: Warner Books, 1990.

Towle, Mike, comp. *True Champions: The Good Guys in American Sports Speak Out*. Forth Worth, TX: The Summit Group, 1994.

Tzu, Sun. *The Art of War,* edited by James Clavell. New York: Dell, 1983.

Walsh, Bill, with Brian Billick and James Peterson. *Bill Walsh: Finding the Winning Edge*. Champaign, IL: Sports Publishers, 1997.

Walton, Gary. *Beyond Winning: The Timeless Wisdom of Great Philosopher Coaches*. Champaign, IL: Human Kinetics Publishers, 1992.

Wooden, John. *They Call Me Coach*. Chicago: NTC Publishing Group, 1988.